INTRODUCTION

The dawn of the automobile age was an exciting time for America, and the classic cars built during those early years were technological marvels both practical and popular.

"It is not outside the realm of possibility that in the century soon to dawn, the horseless carriage may be as familiar on the public highway as the bicycle is today," noted *The San Francisco Call* in February of 1896.

Four years later, they had indeed become more familiar because the motor car trend grew fast. As *The Topeka State Journal* reported at the time, "Among the recent inventions designed for utility, pleasure or comfort, none has attracted so much attention as the automobile."

Of course, all of that attention — not to mention how these new cars made the world so much more accessible — led to a productive multi-million dollar industry. As early as the year 1902, it was estimated that there were 300 different automobile manufacturers in the United States.

On the pages within, we have dozens of classic car brands dating back to the late Victorian age, including Buick, Cadillac, Cartercar, Chalmers, Chandler, Cole, Davis, Ford, Franklin, Grant, Hudson, Kissel, Marmon, Mitchell, Oakland, Oldsmobile, Overland, Packard, Pierce Arrow, Rambler, Scripps-Booth, Stoddard-Dayton and Studebaker. (Note that these images are not modern interpretations of these cars, but authentic illustrations drawn about a century ago to advertise the automobiles or to accompany newspaper stories.)

The drawings are arranged by year, and each of the images on the pages inside was chosen from thousands of illustrations published between 1895 and 1919. They're all printed on just one side of the paper, while page numbering and other image information appears on the reverse, ensuring the coloring side is distraction-free and would even be suitable for framing.

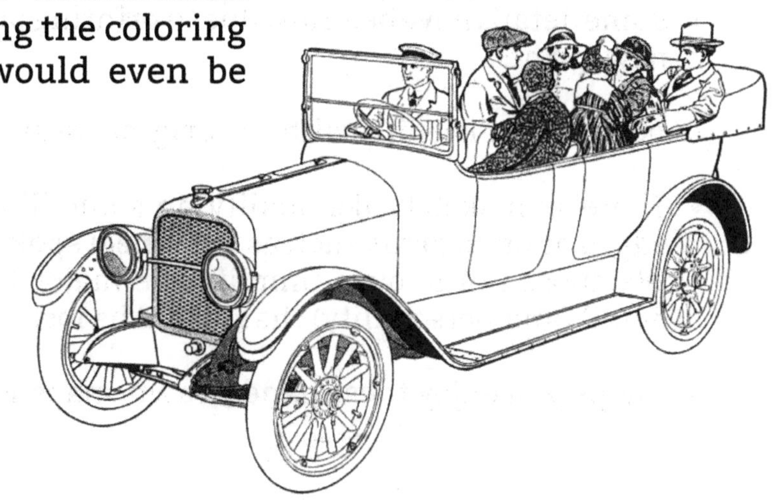

Hope you enjoy the ride!

Nancy J. Price
Founder, Click Americana
Editor-in-Chief, Myria.com

IMPORTANT NOTES

Within these covers, dozens of authentic vintage automobile illustrations have been rediscovered and transformed into coloring pages. Every one of the retro images in this book was carefully chosen, then painstakingly restored by hand using modern technology in order to return it to its original glory as much as possible.

Before creating this collection, we reached out to coloring book fans, and incorporated as many of their suggestions as we could:

- Each detailed retro picture is printed only on one side of the paper, allowing you to color with your choice of medium without worrying about bleed-through to an image on the back. (If you like, slip a blank page from the end of the book behind the picture you're coloring to avoid ink or paint bleeding onto the next illustration.)
- Page numbering, titles and other image information appears on the reverse of each page, ensuring the coloring side is distraction-free and suitable for framing.

Although these pictures were not created with colored pens, pencils, crayons or paints in mind, we reviewed hundreds of drawings to select those most suited to the task. Still, due to the authentic vintage nature of the artwork, this isn't a typical adult coloring book of modern images with pristine lines.

The images were restored as faithfully as possible, but since the original artwork is not known to exist, we relied upon high-resolution scans of the printed newspaper pages. As such, there are a few caveats:

- Some illustrations have areas of black, including in backgrounds, stripes and other design elements.
- Borders, shapes and lines are occasionally incomplete.
- Some details have been lost due to printing processes and quality of preserved newsprint.

In addition, in keeping with the original designs, you will also see...

- There's an sketch-like quality on some illustrations, particularly near the edges or on in areas such as the wheel spokes.
- We chose not to over-simplify the majority of the artwork because of the detail (and personality) that would be lost in the process.

We hope you enjoy these hand-drawn snapshots of history in the making!

CLICK AMERICANA® PRESENTS

CLASSIC CARS ADULT COLORING BOOK #1

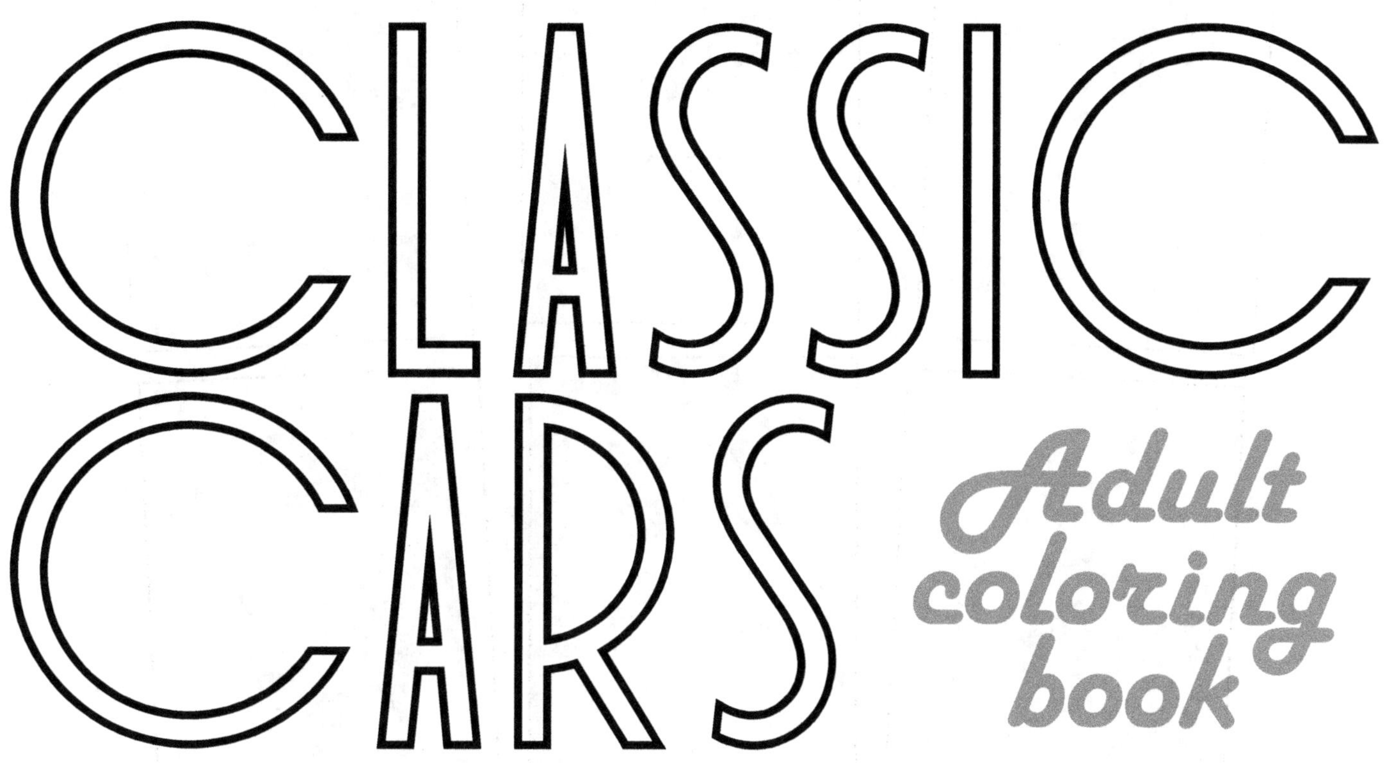

EARLY AMERICAN AUTOMOBILES: 1895-1919

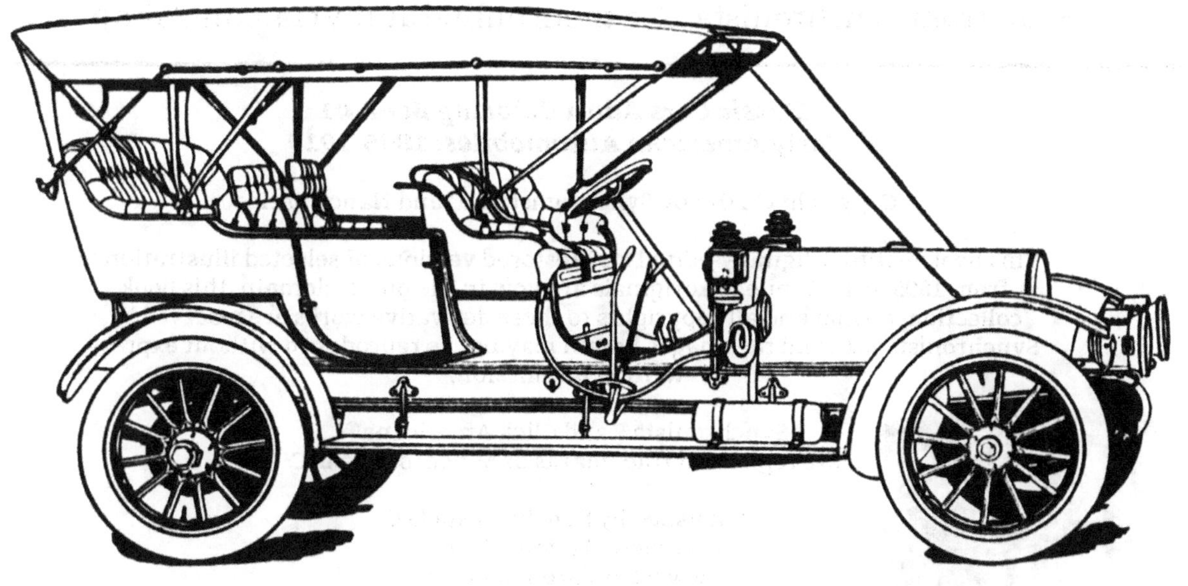

FROM THE EDITORS OF CLICK AMERICANA®
CLICKAMERICANA.COM

INTRODUCTION BY NANCY J. PRICE
EDITOR-IN-CHIEF, MYRIA.COM

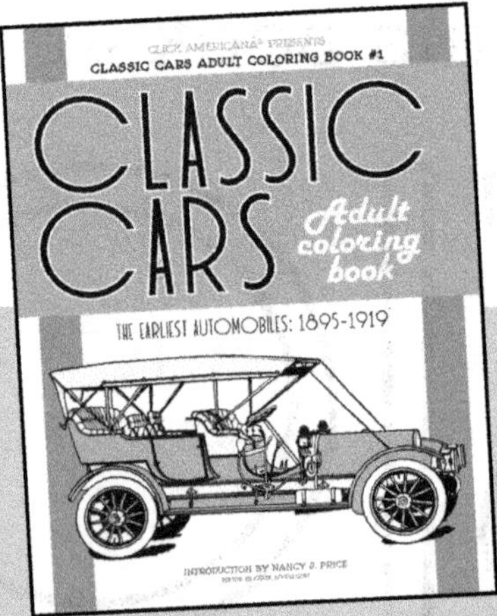

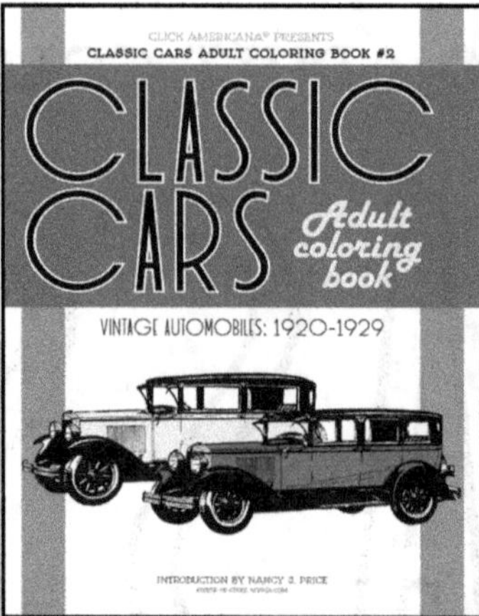

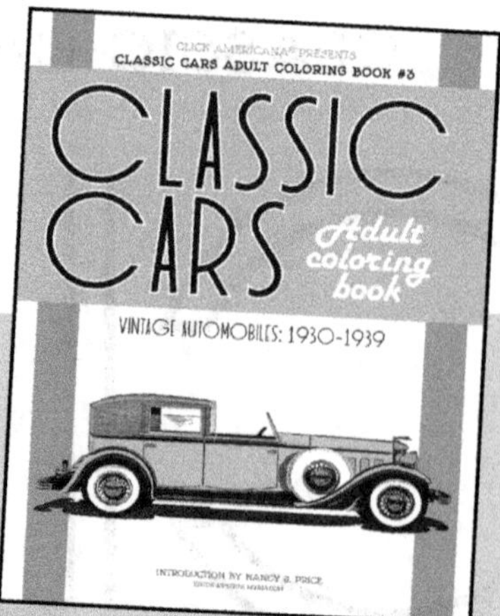

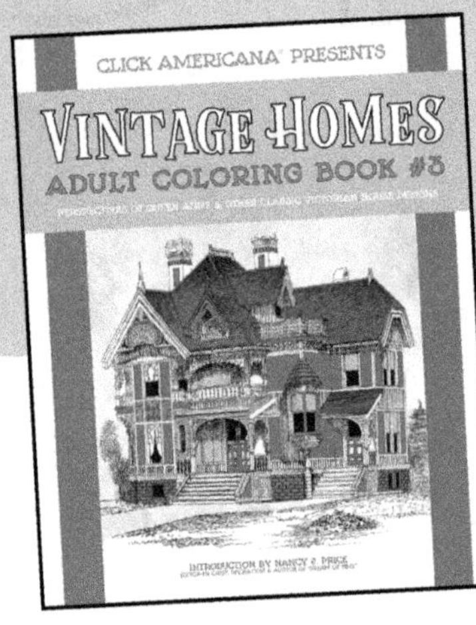

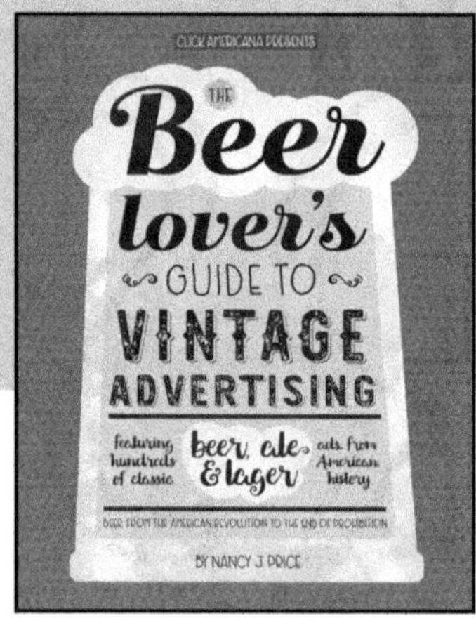

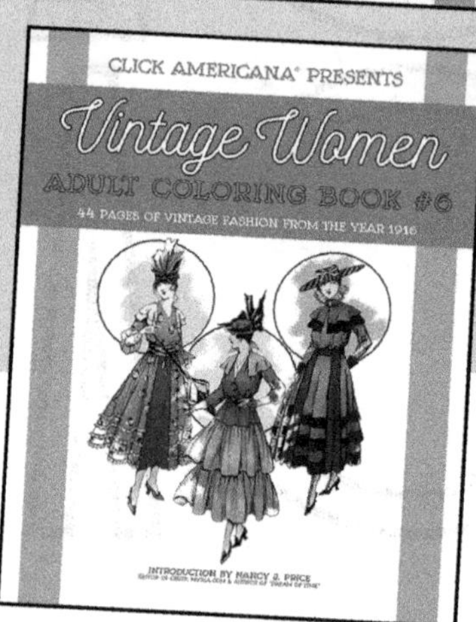

Check out our other books, including
Vintage Homes Adult Coloring Books, Vintage Women Adult Coloring Books
and *the Beer Lover's Guide to Vintage Advertising*
— all from Synchronista. See them online at myria.com/shop

Classic Cars Adult Coloring Book #1
Early American Automobiles: 1895-1919

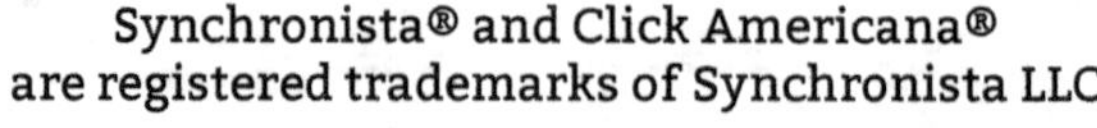

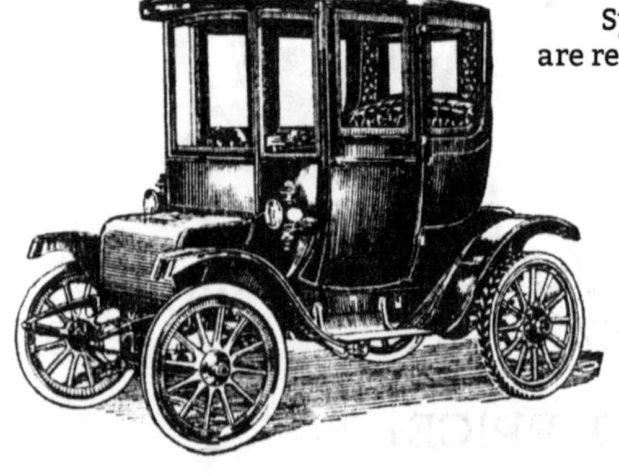

Published by Synchronista LLC
Gilbert, Arizona, USA
www.Synchronista.com

See more books at
ClickAmericana.com/shop

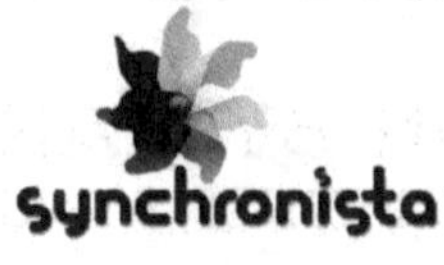

WELCOME!

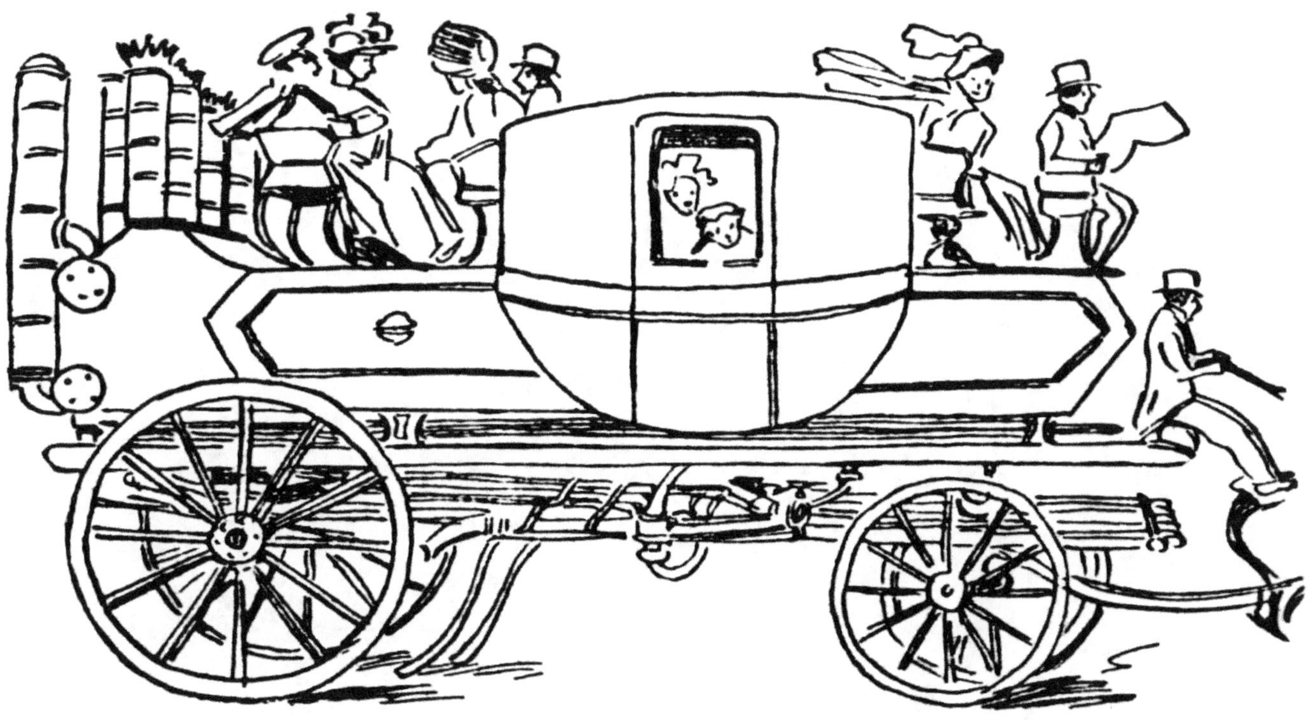

**"There is no new thing under the sun;
An English horseless carriage of 1827 and thought to be the earliest one."**

As seen in *The Philadelphia Inquirer* (Pennsylvania)
November 17, 1895

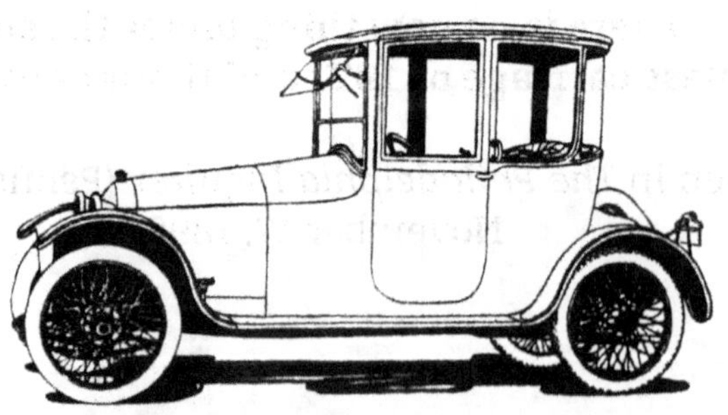

Tip: Find the details about the following illustrations in this space on the back of each page

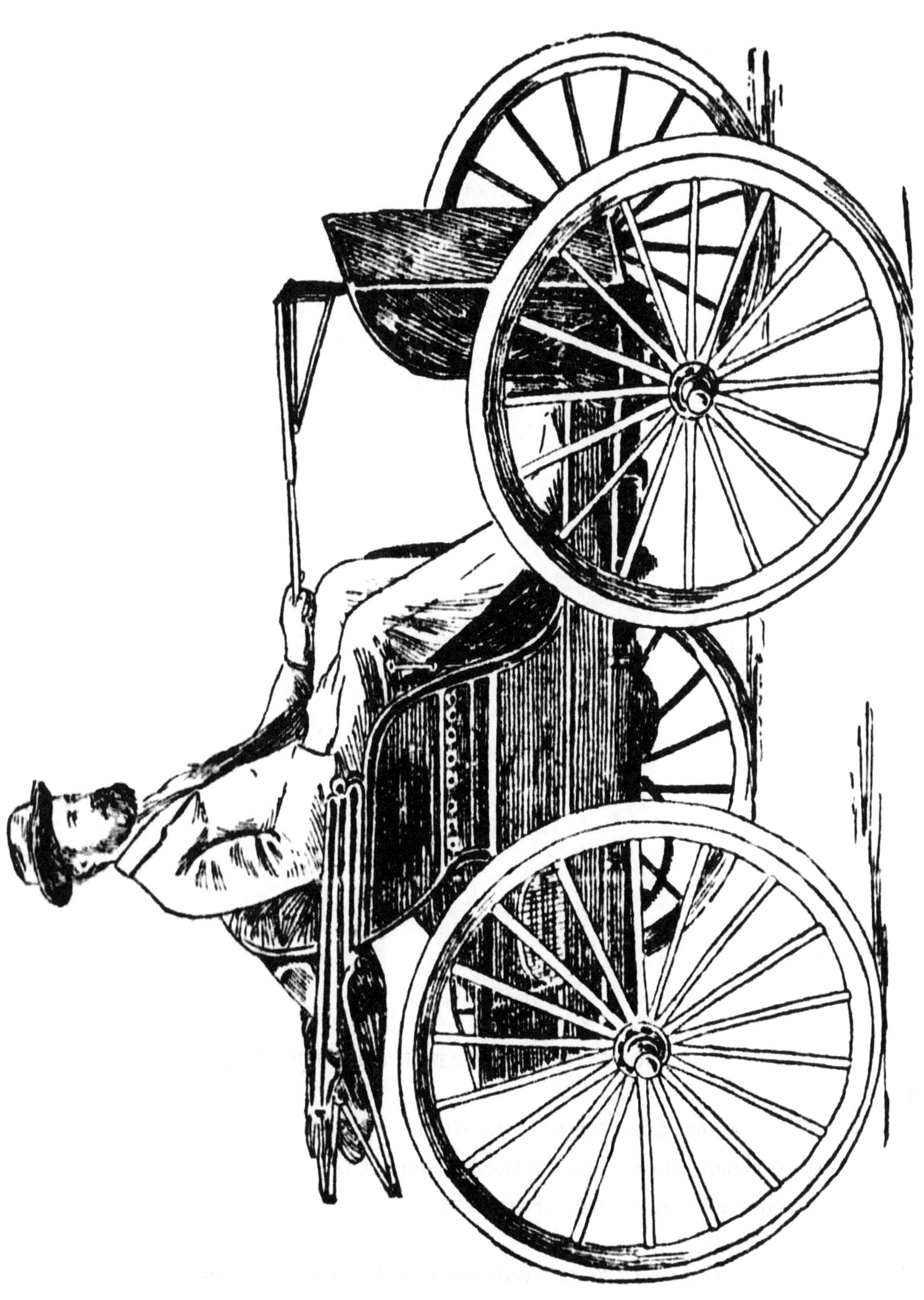

ABOUT THE ILLUSTRATION ON THE REVERSE

Automobile:	Duryea Motor Wagon
Original publication:	Evening Star (Washington DC)
Publication date:	December 3, 1895

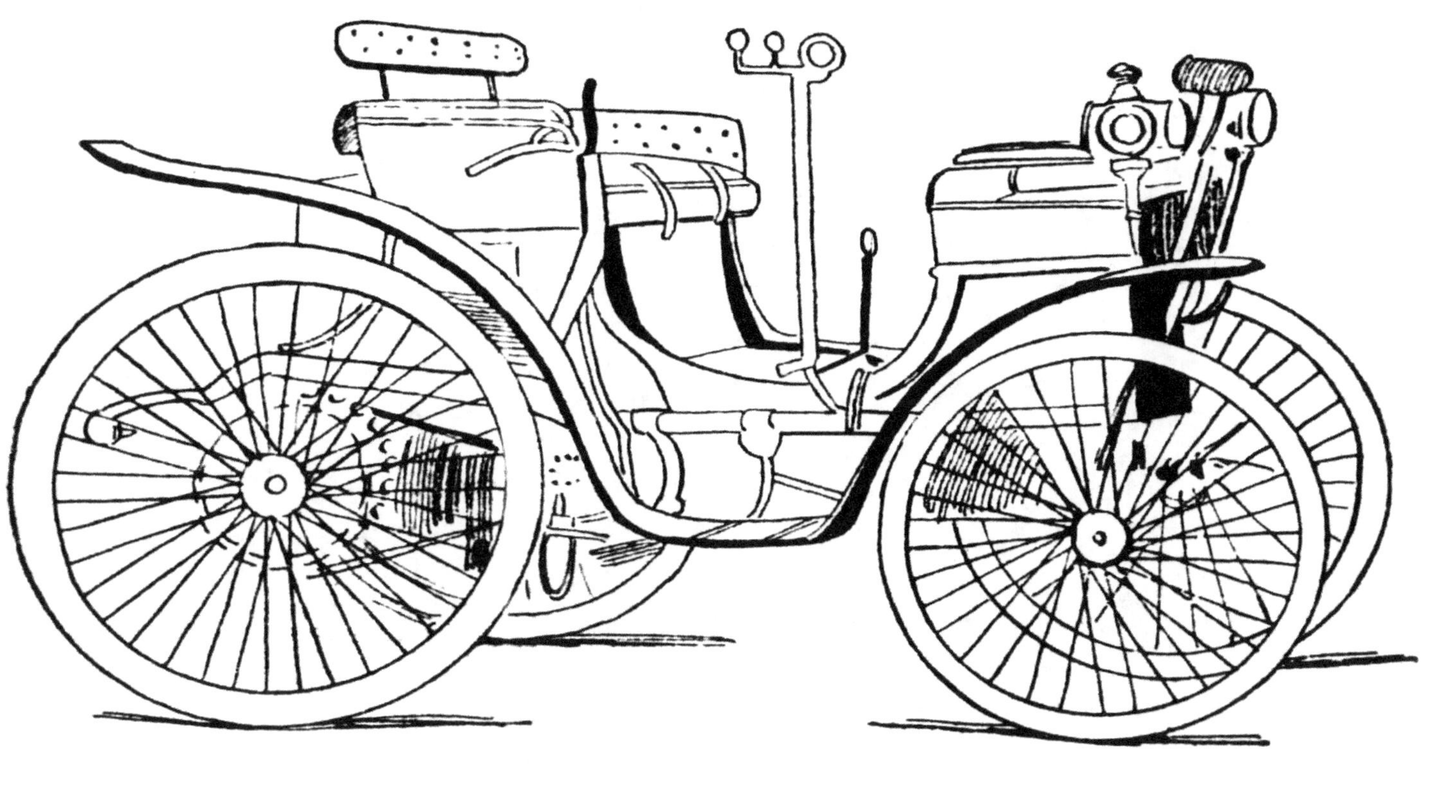

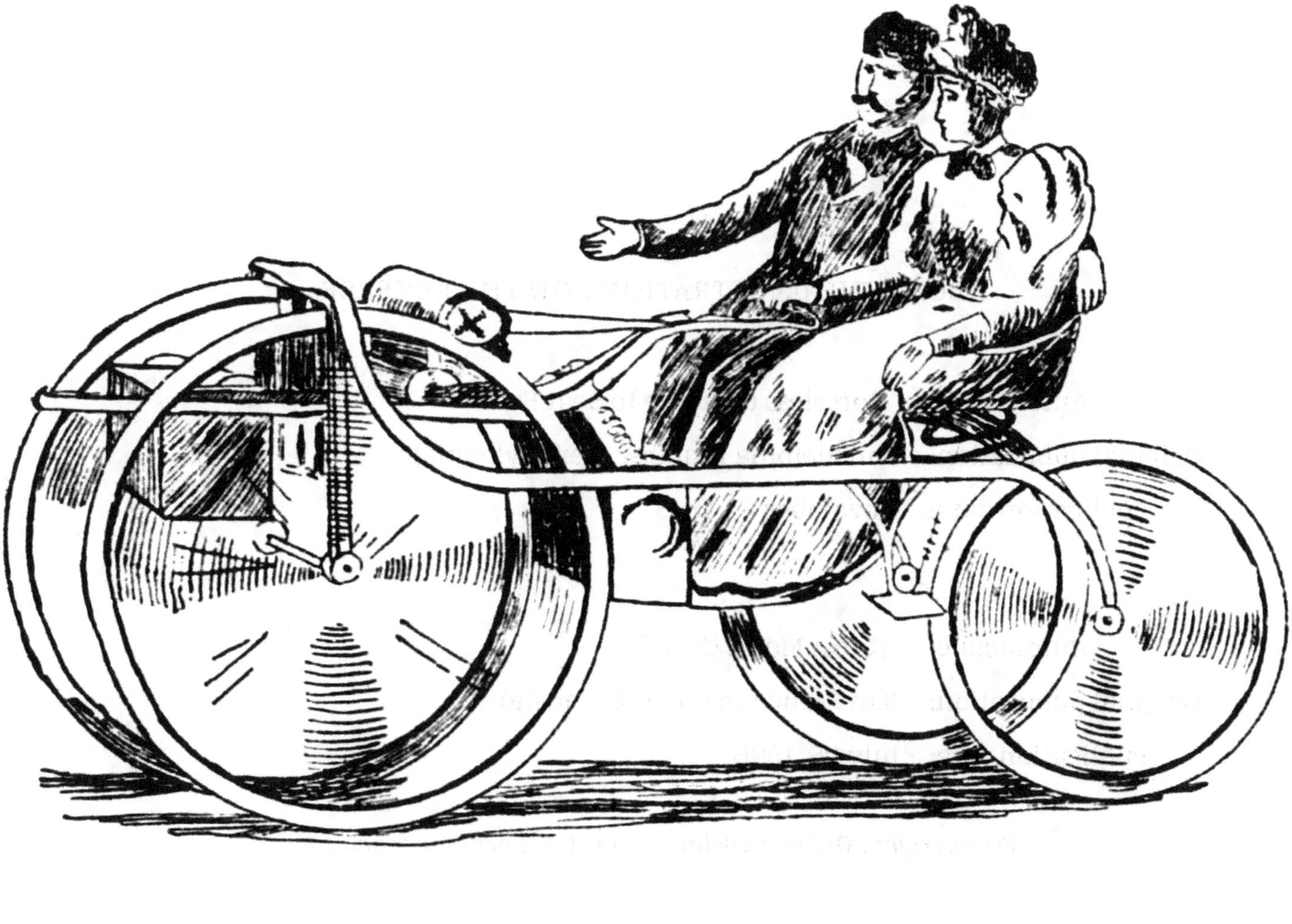

ABOUT THE ILLUSTRATIONS ON THE REVERSE

Automobile:	"Horseless Carriage to Seat Four"
Original publication:	Philadelphia Inquirer (Pennsylvania)
Publication date:	November 17, 1895

Automobile:	"Latest Motor Cycle"
Original publication:	San Francisco Call (California)
Publication date:	July 05, 1896

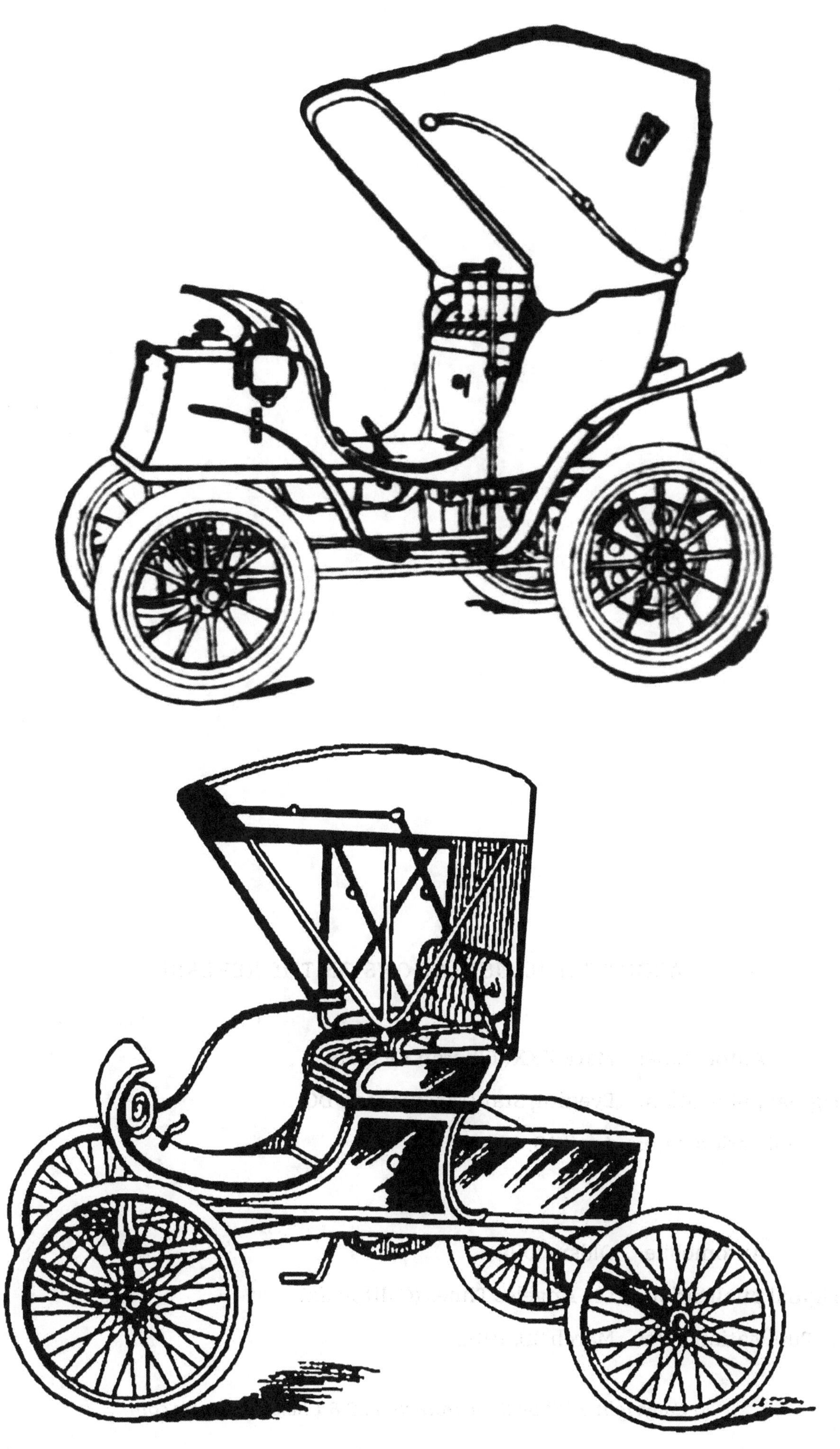

ABOUT THE ILLUSTRATIONS ON THE REVERSE

Automobile:	Mark XXXI Elberon Victoria
Original publication:	Evening Star (Washington DC)
Publication date:	April 10, 1902

Automobile:	Oldsmobile
Original publication:	Los Angeles Times (California)
Publication date:	March 30, 1902

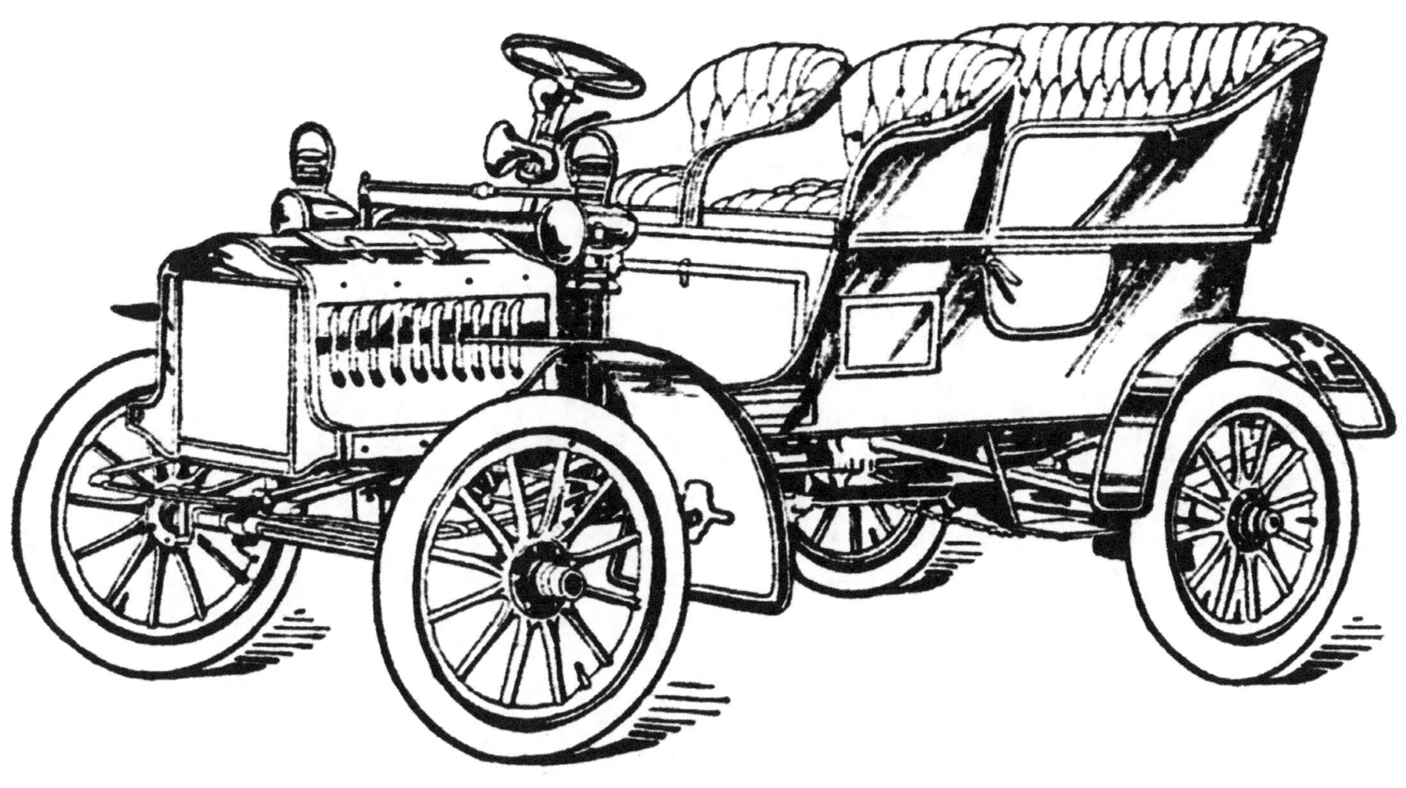

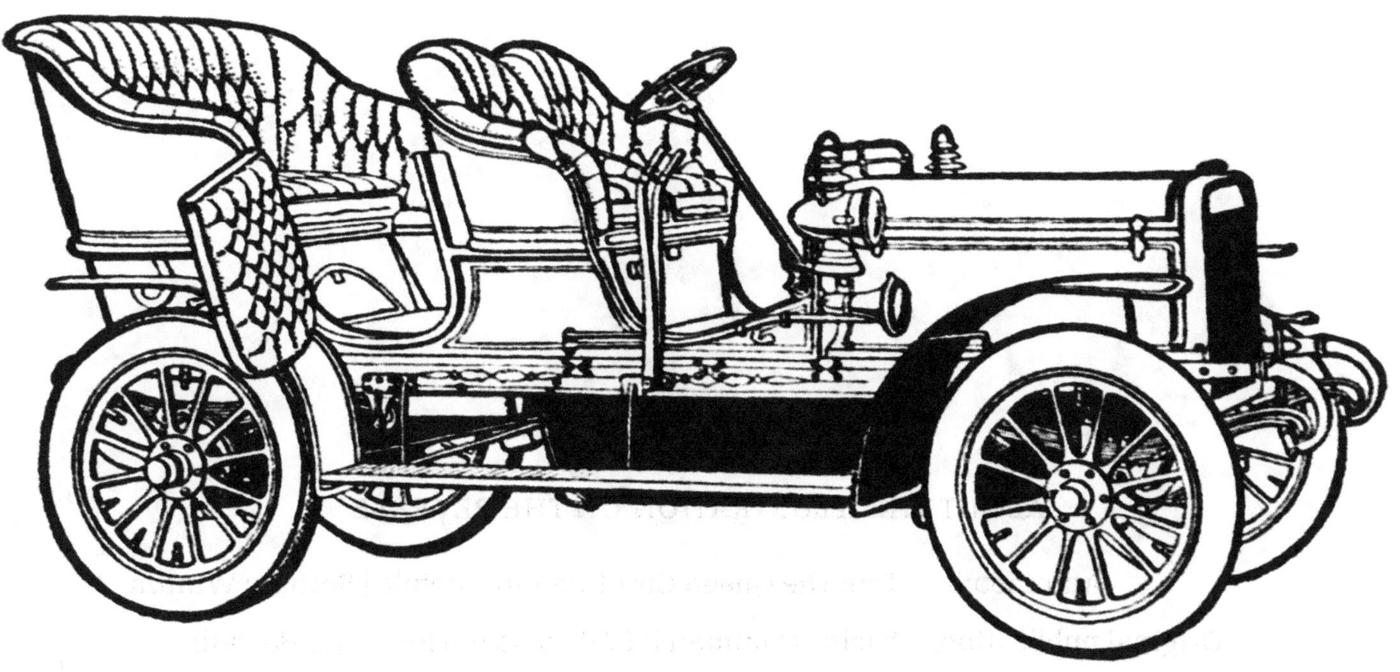

ABOUT THE ILLUSTRATION ON THE REVERSE

Automobile:	Top: The Queen Gasoline Automobile | Bottom: Winton
Original publication:	Pacific Commercial Advertiser (Honolulu, Hawaii)
Publication date:	July 23, 1905

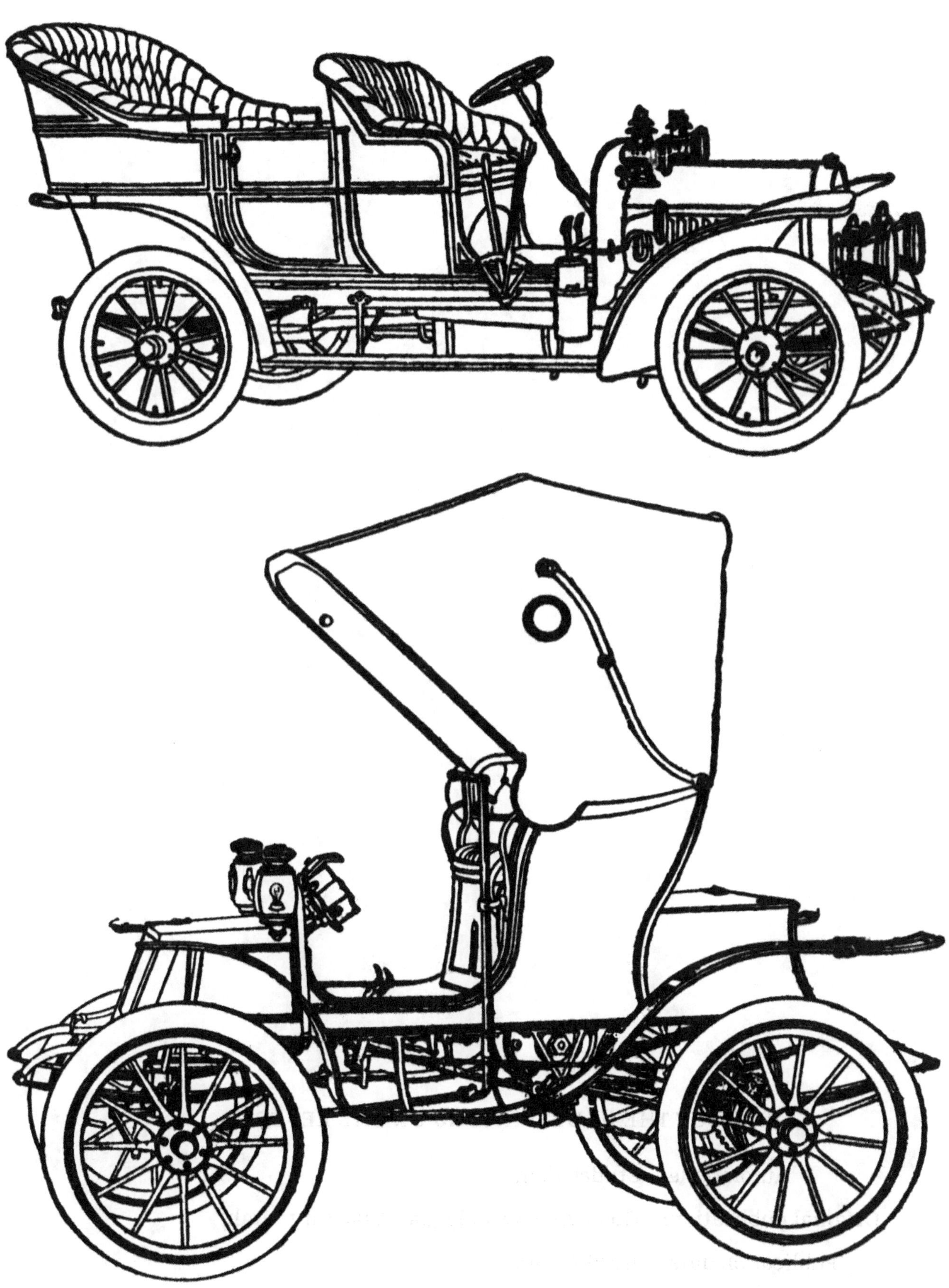

ABOUT THE ILLUSTRATIONS ON THE REVERSE

Automobile:	Studebakers
Original publication:	Goodwin's Weekly (Salt Lake City, Utah)
Publication date:	April 7, 1906

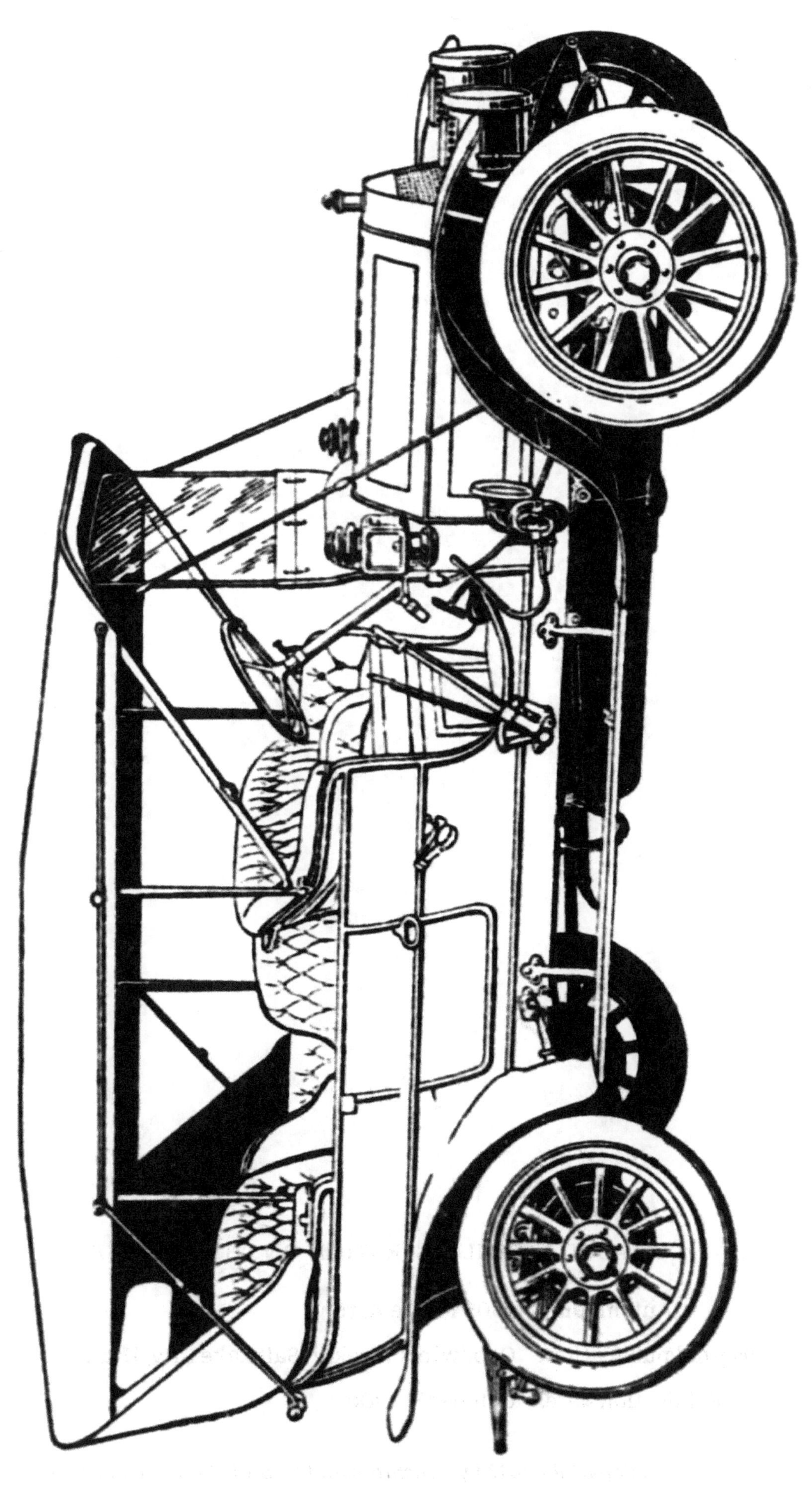

ABOUT THE ILLUSTRATION ON THE REVERSE

Automobile:	1909 Pierce Arrow
Original publication:	Goodwin's Weekly (Salt Lake City, Utah)
Publication date:	October 3, 1908

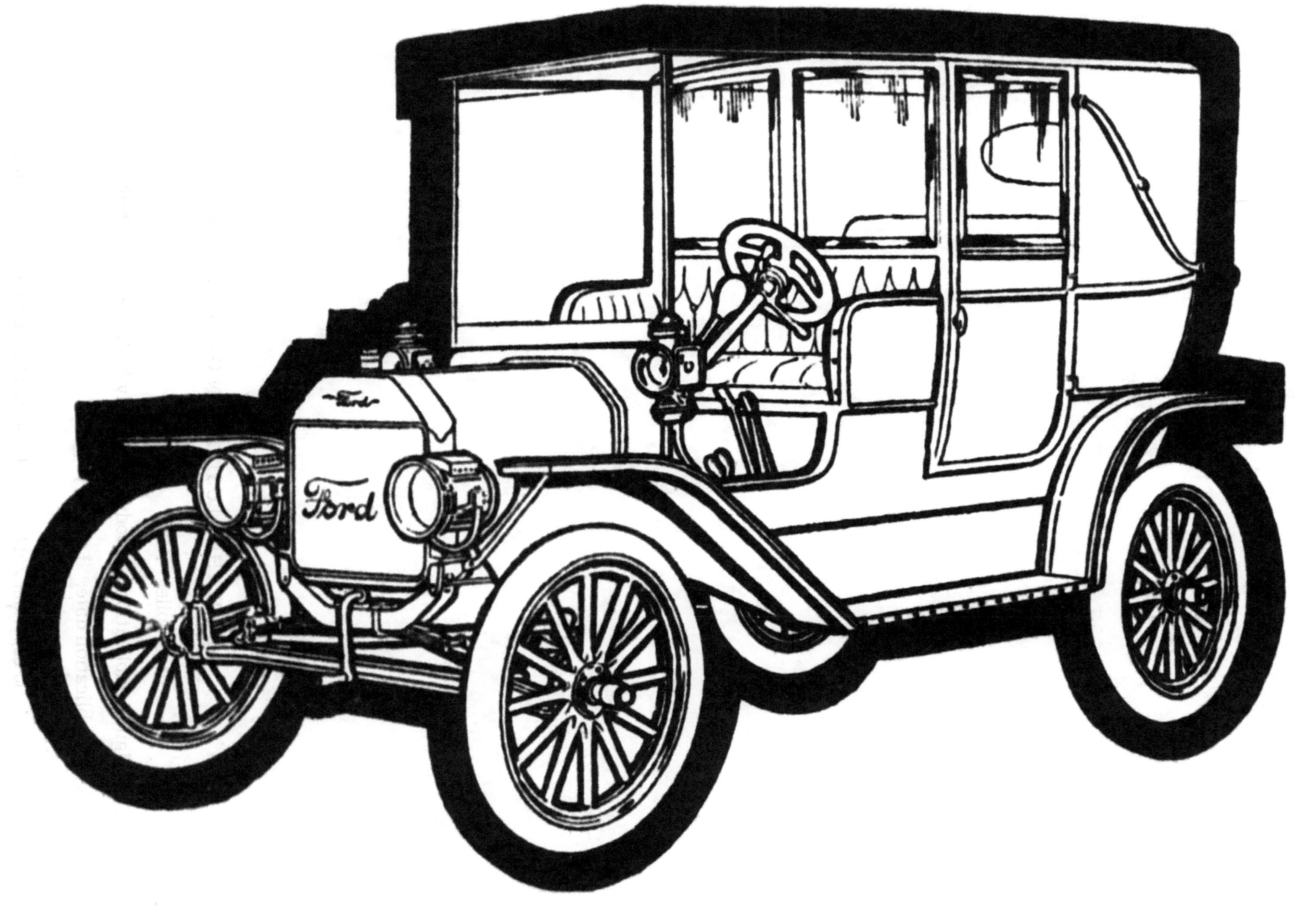
Ford

ABOUT THE ILLUSTRATION ON THE REVERSE

Automobile:	Ford
Original publication:	Goodwin's Weekly (Salt Lake City, Utah)
Publication date:	February 6, 1909

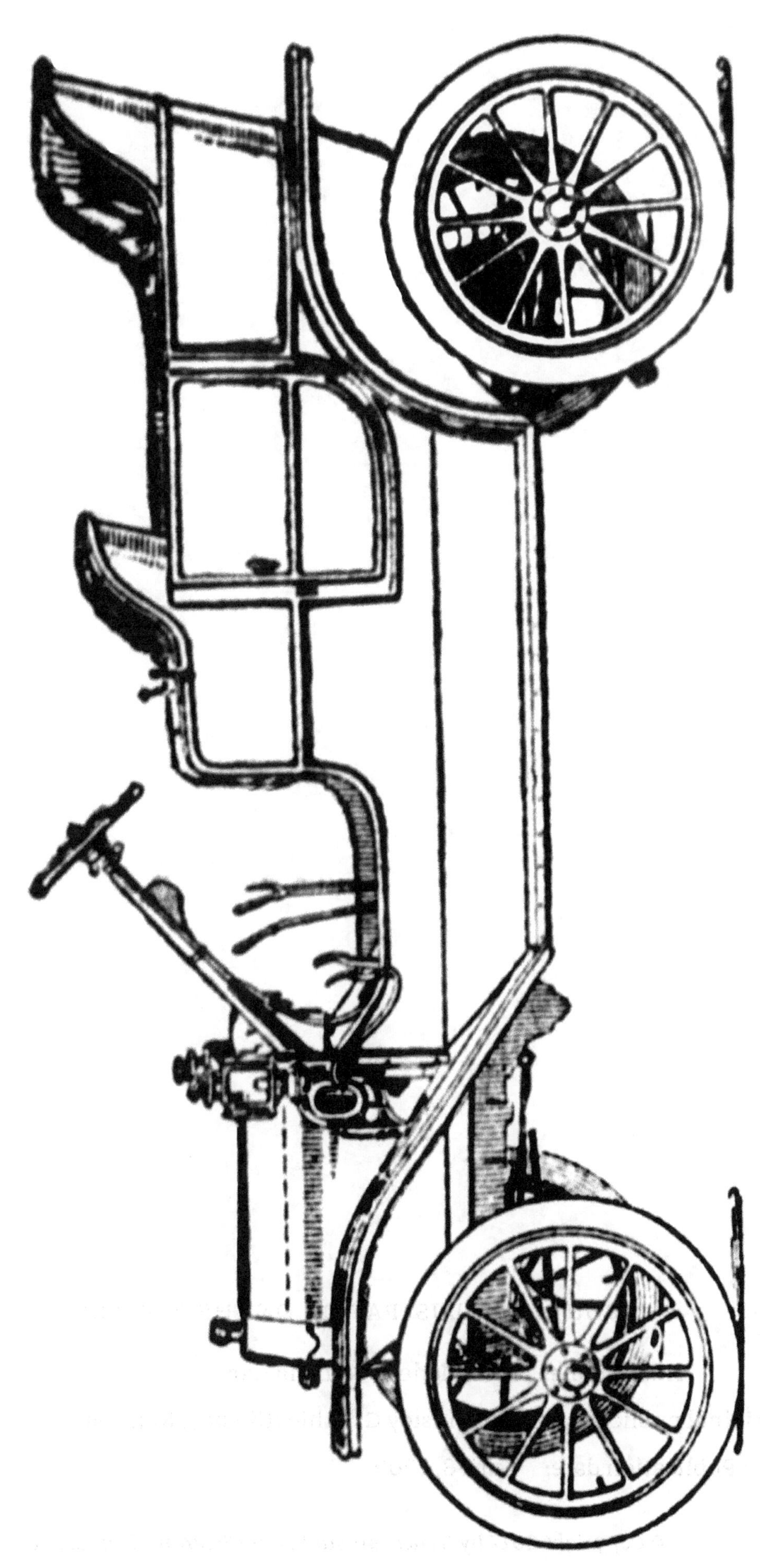

ABOUT THE ILLUSTRATION ON THE REVERSE

Automobile:	Ford Model T Touring Car
Original publication:	The Kinsley Graphic (Kinsley, Kansas)
Publication date:	April 8, 1909

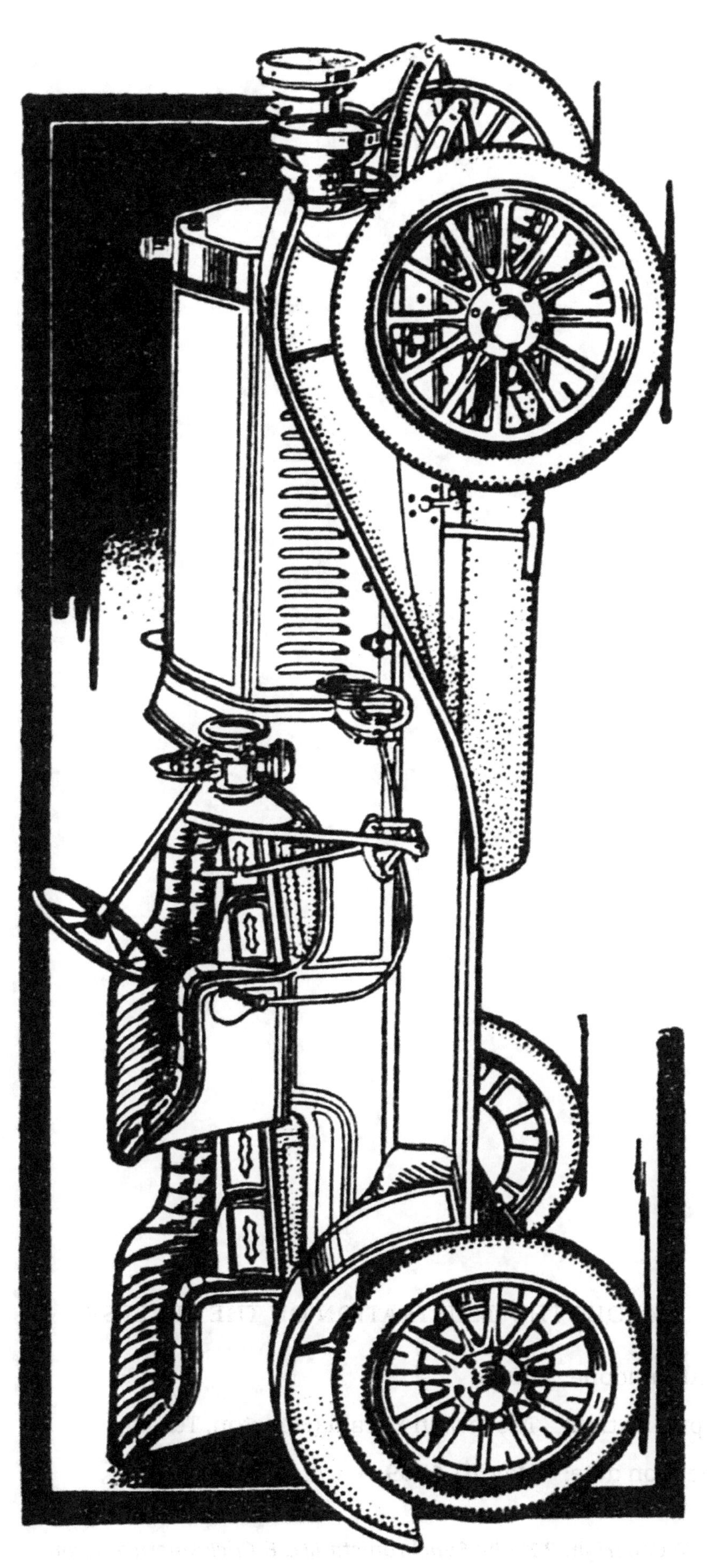

ABOUT THE ILLUSTRATION ON THE REVERSE

Automobile: Buick

Original publication: The Jewish Herald (Houston, Texas)

Publication date: May 20, 1909

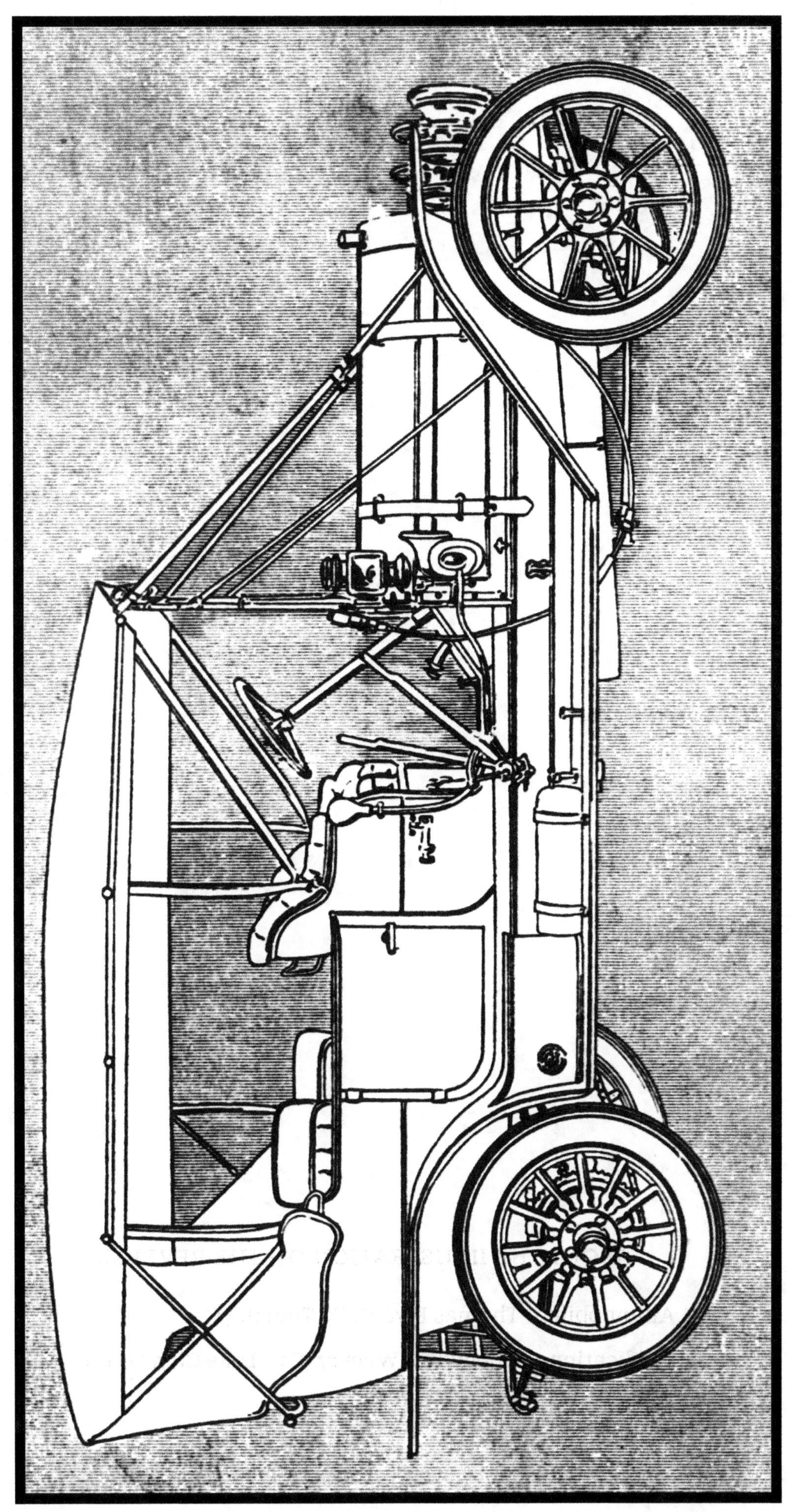

ABOUT THE ILLUSTRATION ON THE REVERSE

Automobile:	Thomas Flyer 6-70 Touring Car
Original publication:	Goodwin's Weekly (Salt Lake City, Utah)
Publication date:	June 19, 1909

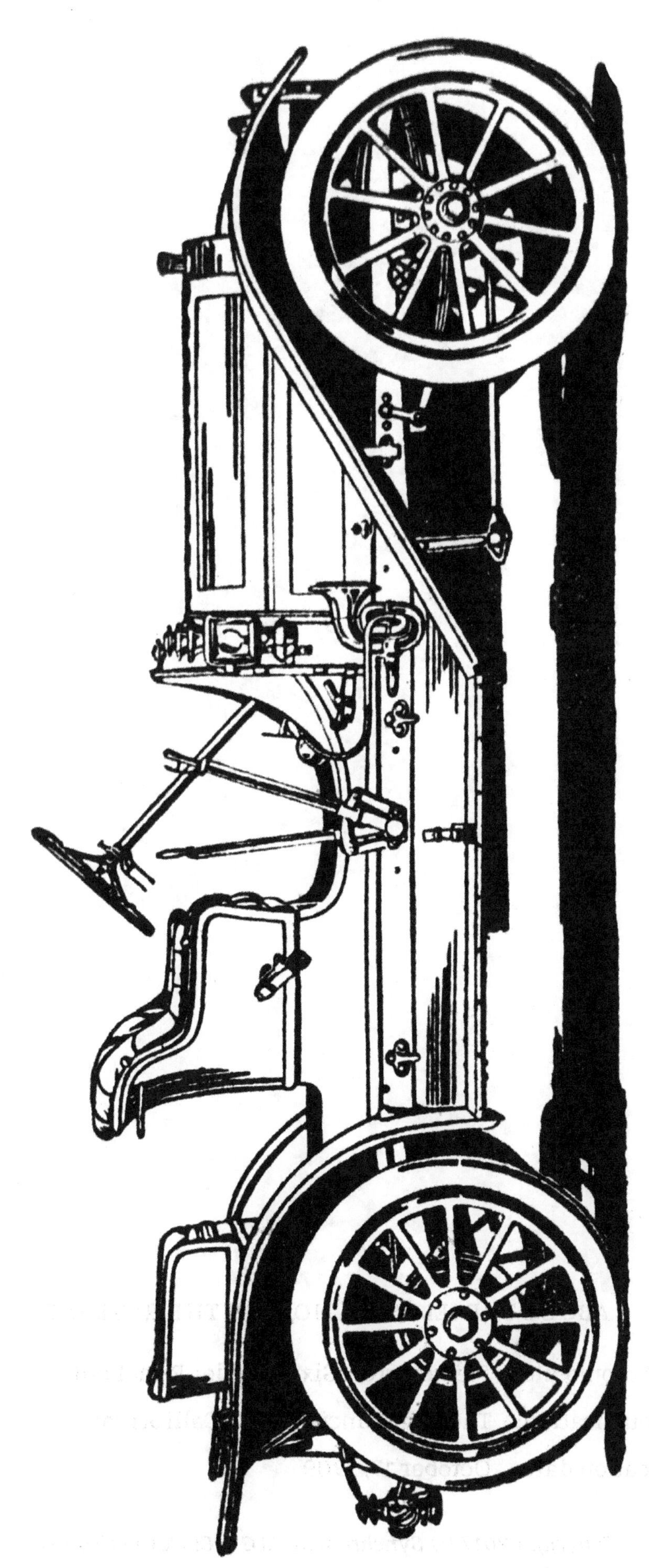

ABOUT THE ILLUSTRATION ON THE REVERSE

Automobile:	Pierce Arrow Six-Cylinder Runabout
Original publication:	The San Francisco Call (California)
Publication date:	October 17, 1909

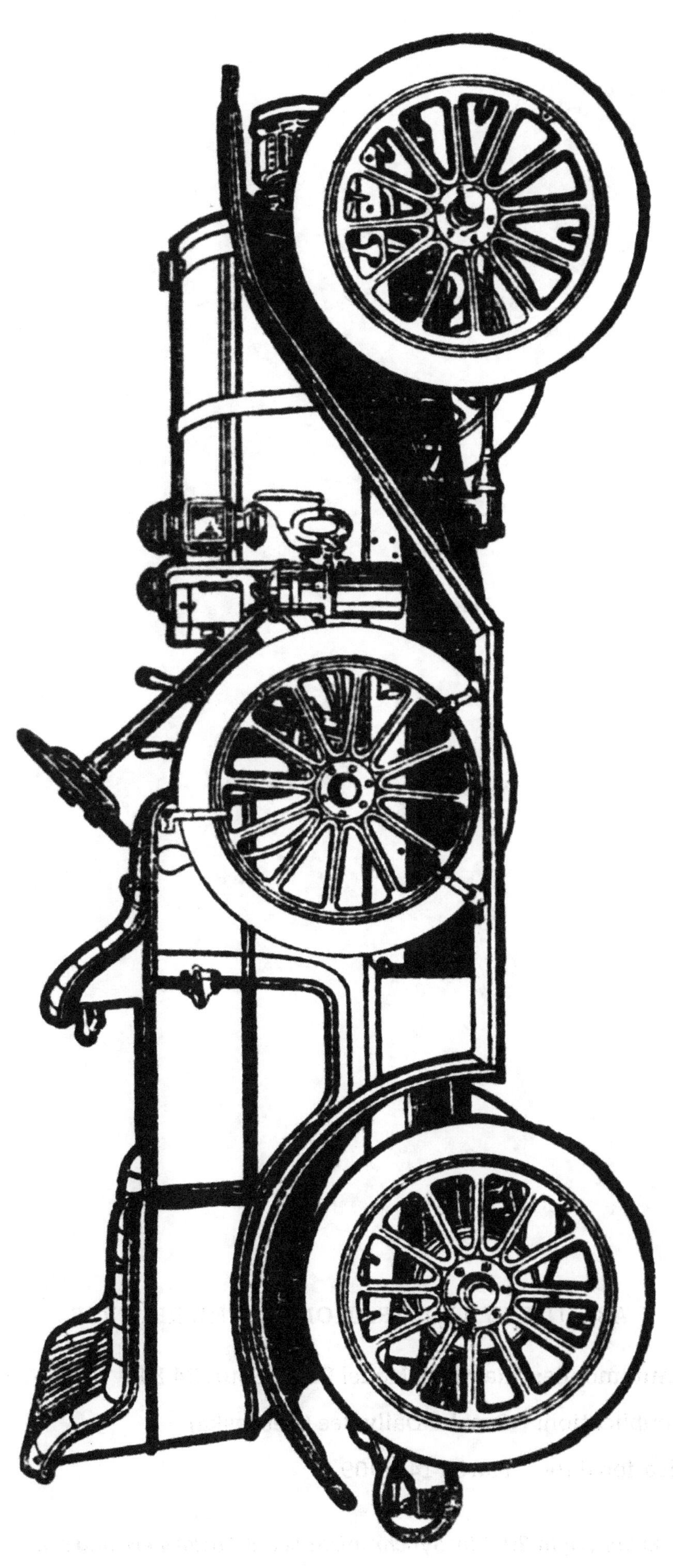

ABOUT THE ILLUSTRATION ON THE REVERSE

Automobile:	Rambler Model Forty-Four, 34 HP
Original publication:	Omaha Daily Bee (Nebraska)
Publication date:	March 14, 1909

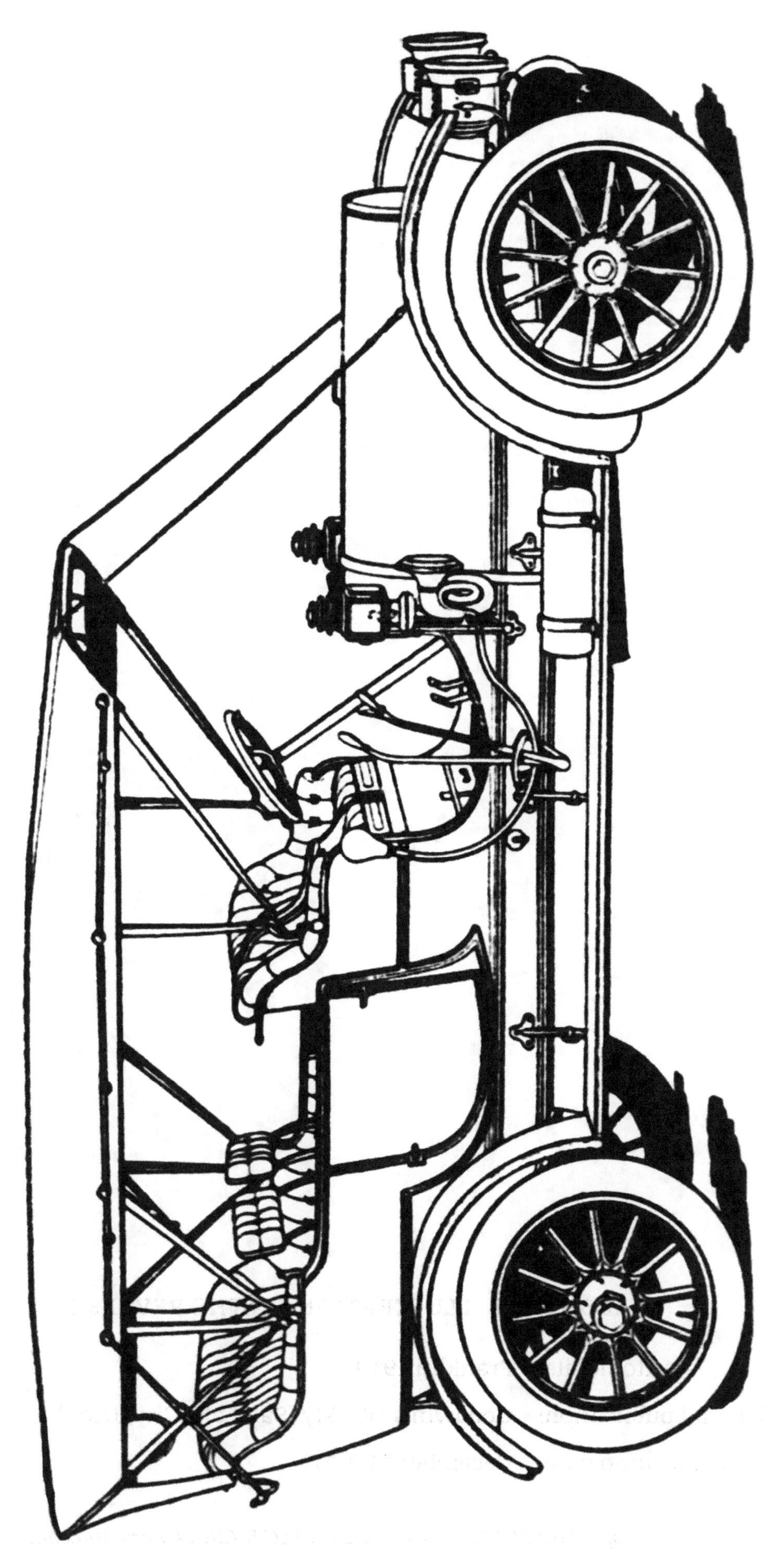

ABOUT THE ILLUSTRATION ON THE REVERSE

Automobile: Franklin 1910

Original publication: Goodwin's Weekly (Salt Lake City, Utah)

Publication date: December 11, 1909

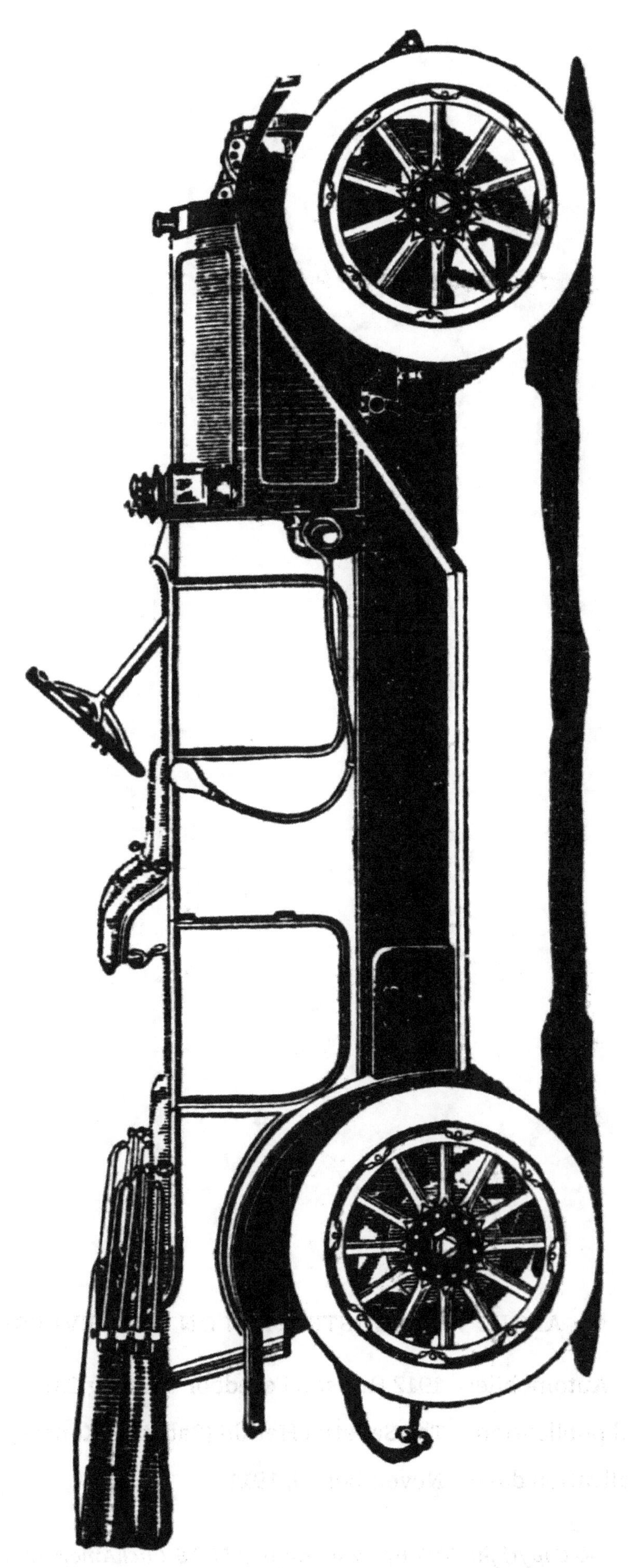

ABOUT THE ILLUSTRATION ON THE REVERSE

Automobile: 1912 Hudson Foredoor Touring Car

Original publication: The Sabetha Herald (Sabetha, Kansas)

Publication date: November 23, 1911

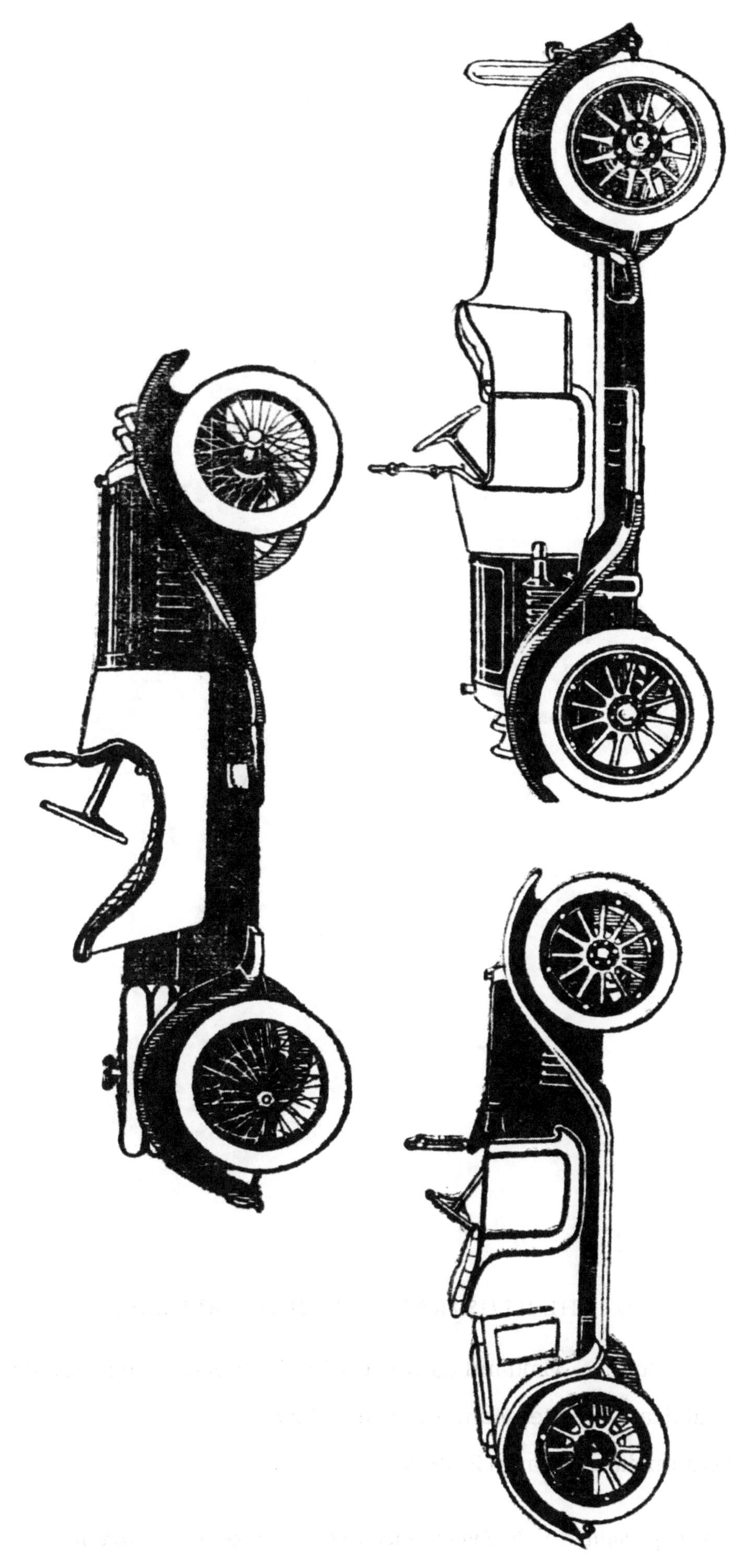

ABOUT THE ILLUSTRATIONS ON THE REVERSE

Automobile:	Oakland Cars: 6-60 Roadster, 35 Sociable Roadster, 42 Roadster
Original publication:	Des Moines Register (Iowa)
Publication date:	March 2, 1913

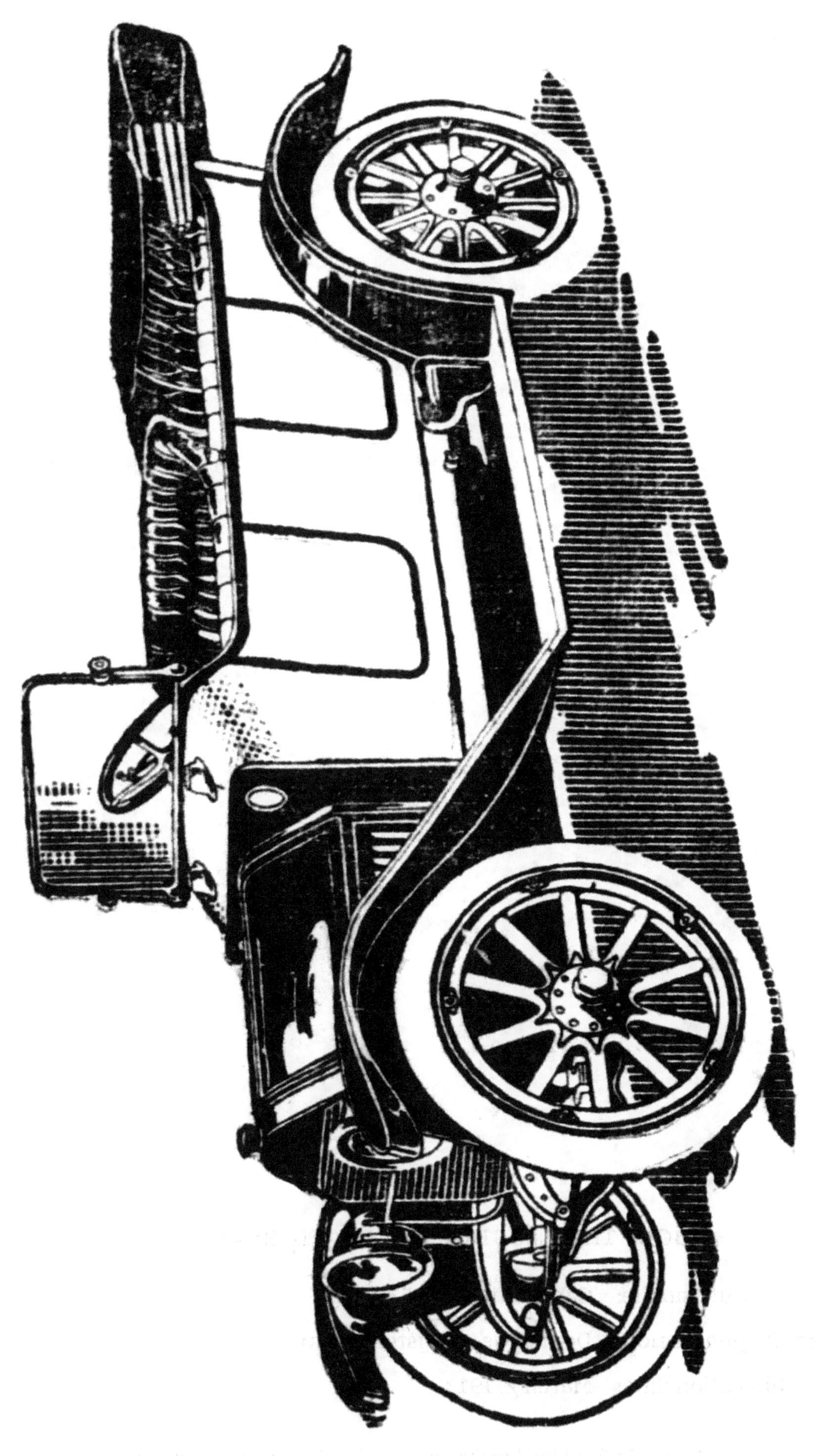

ABOUT THE ILLUSTRATION ON THE REVERSE

Automobile:	Cartercar Model 5A
Original publication:	Des Moines Register (Iowa)
Publication date:	March 2, 1913

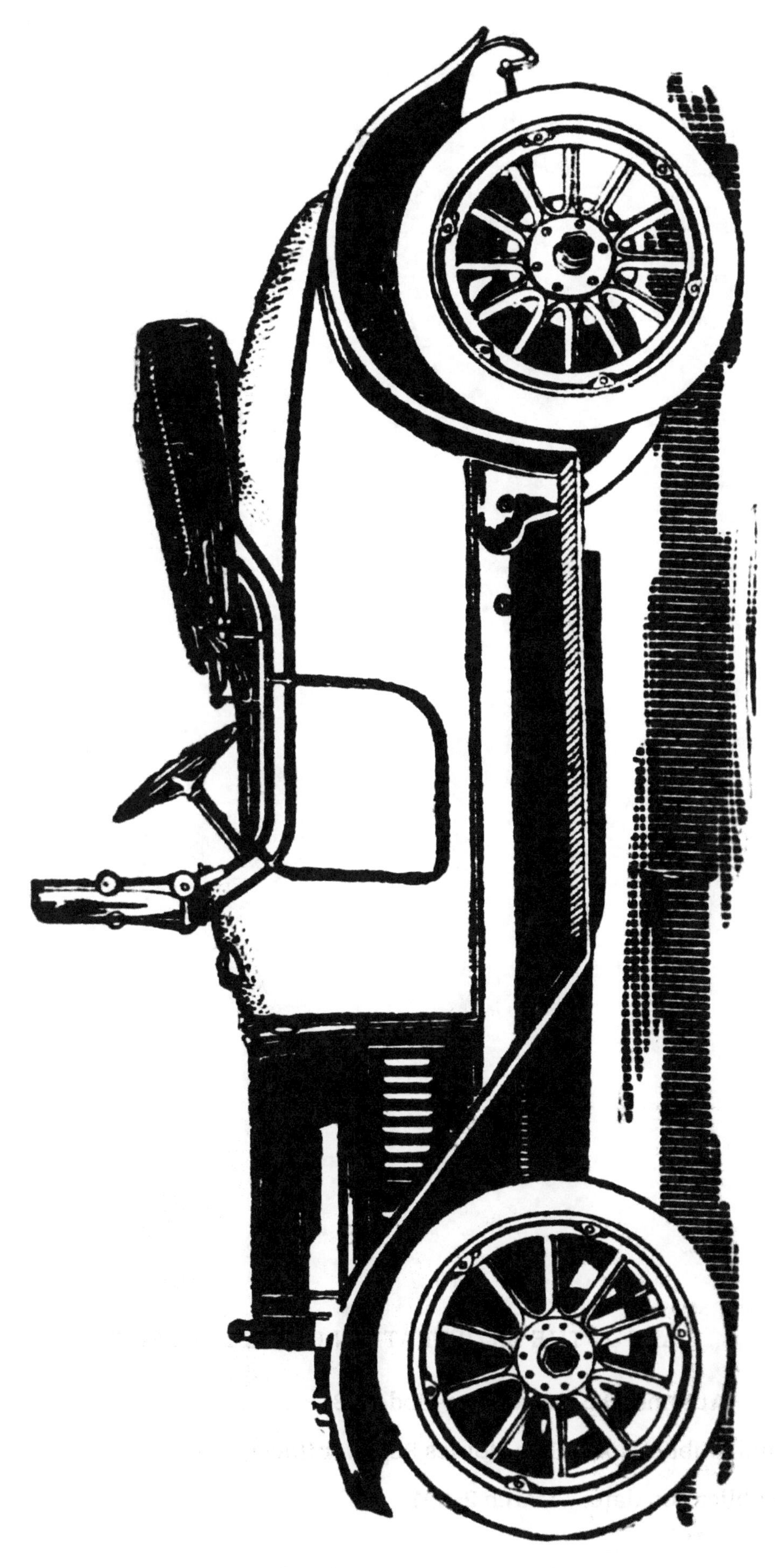

ABOUT THE ILLUSTRATION ON THE REVERSE

Automobile:	Cartercar Model 5B
Original publication:	Des Moines Register (Iowa)
Publication date:	March 2, 1913

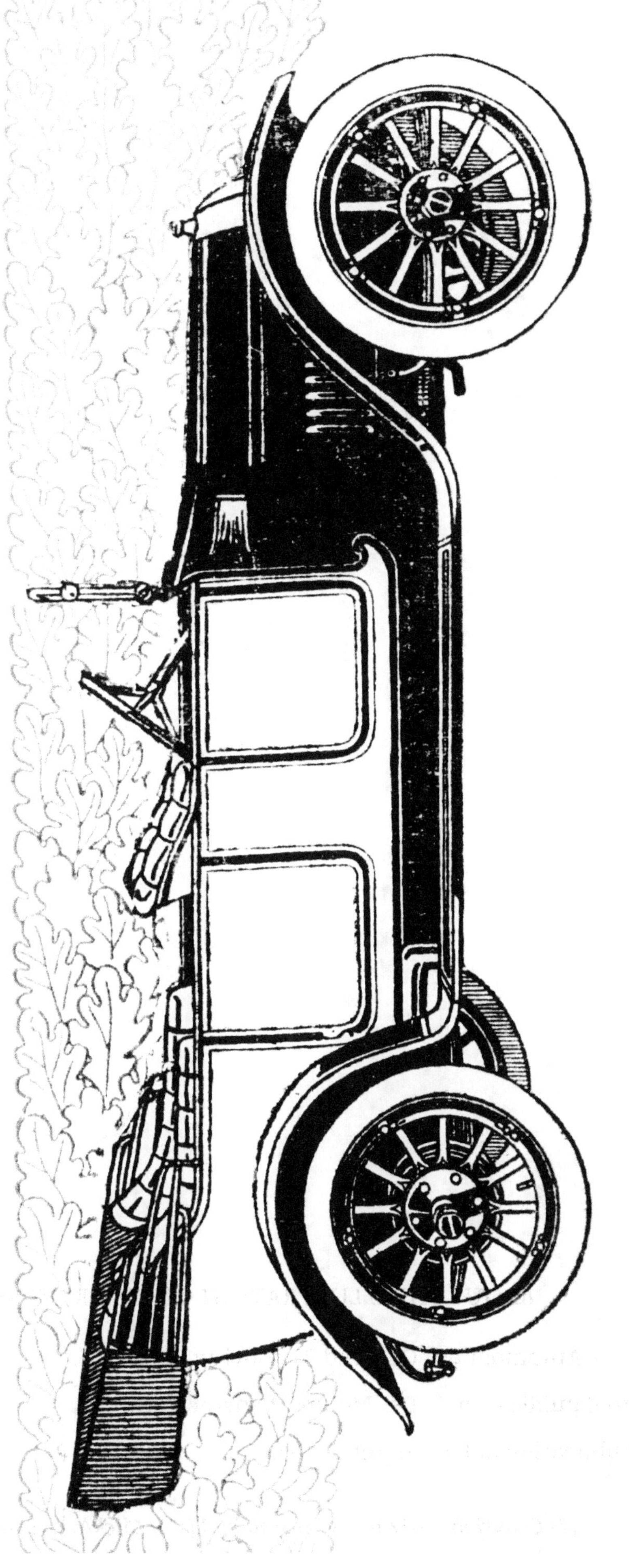

ABOUT THE ILLUSTRATION ON THE REVERSE

Automobile:	Oakland 35 Touring Car
Original publication:	Des Moines Register (Iowa)
Publication date:	March 2, 1913

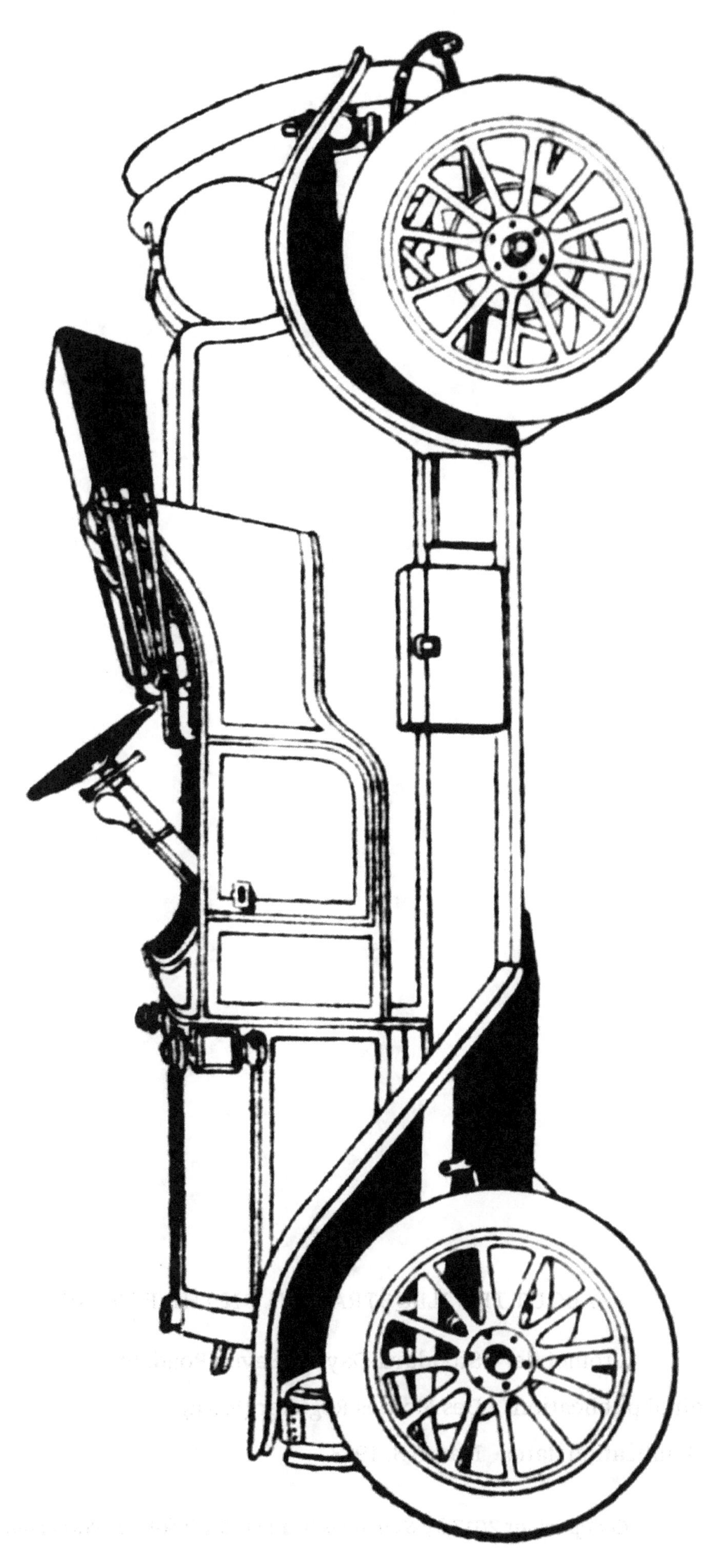

ABOUT THE ILLUSTRATION ON THE REVERSE

Automobile:	Stoddard-Dayton Savoy Roadster
Original publication:	Des Moines Register (Iowa)
Publication date:	March 3, 1913

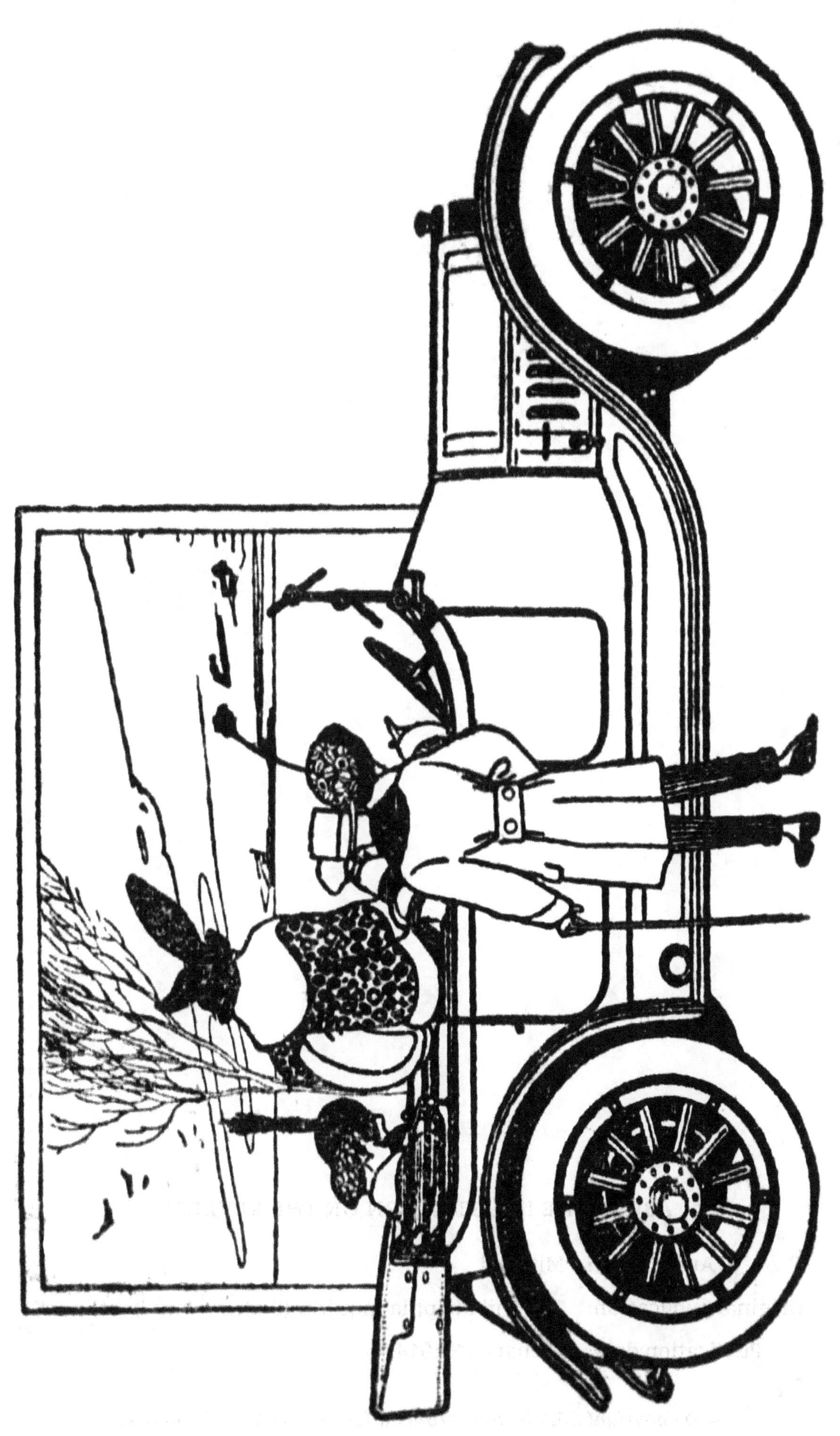

ABOUT THE ILLUSTRATION ON THE REVERSE

Automobile: Mitchell

Original publication: The Philadelphia Inquirer (Pennsylvania)

Publication date: January 11, 1914

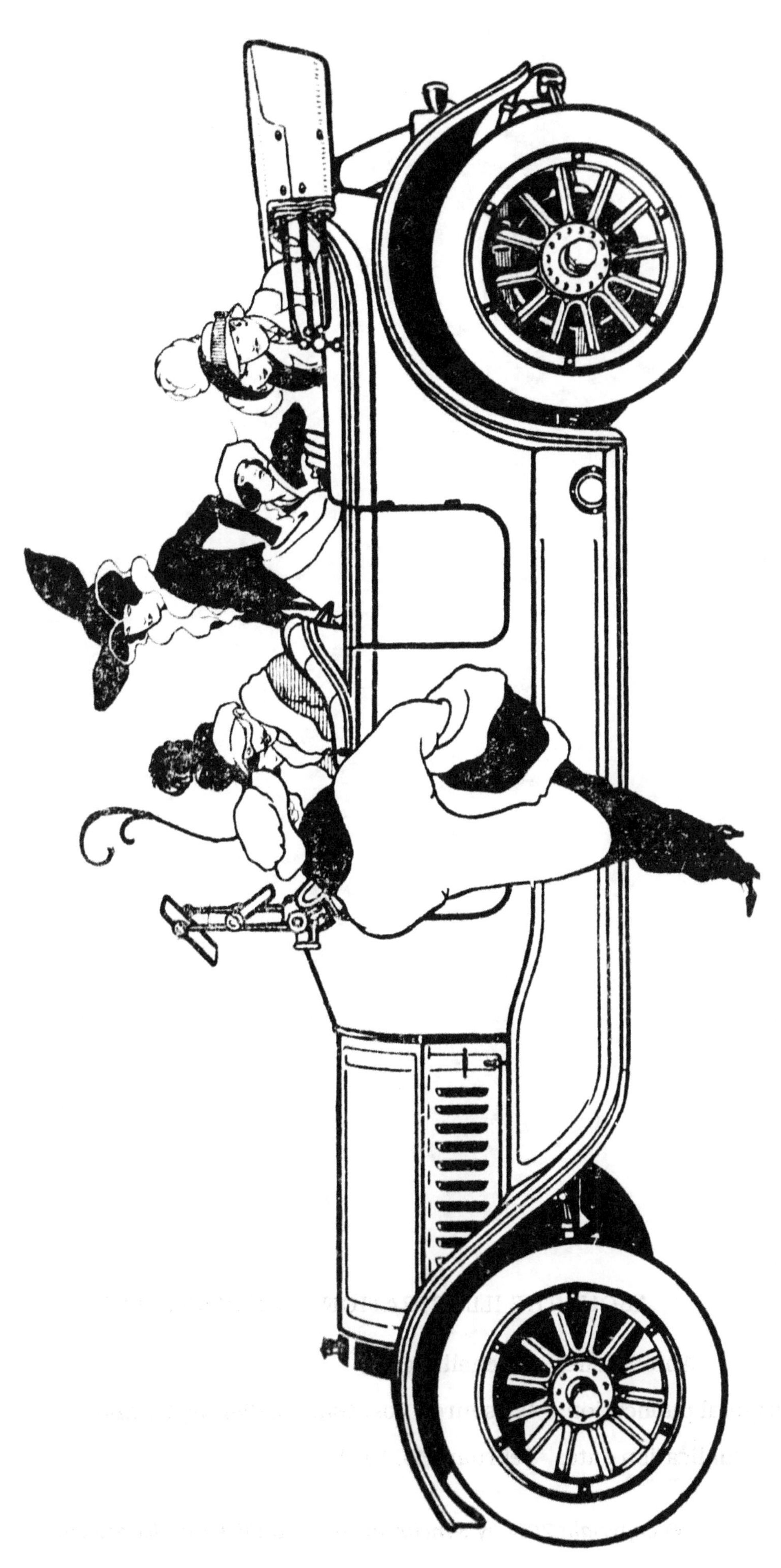

ABOUT THE ILLUSTRATION ON THE REVERSE

Automobile:	Mitchell Big Six
Original publication:	Pittsburgh Post Gazette (Pennsylvania)
Publication date:	February 15, 1914

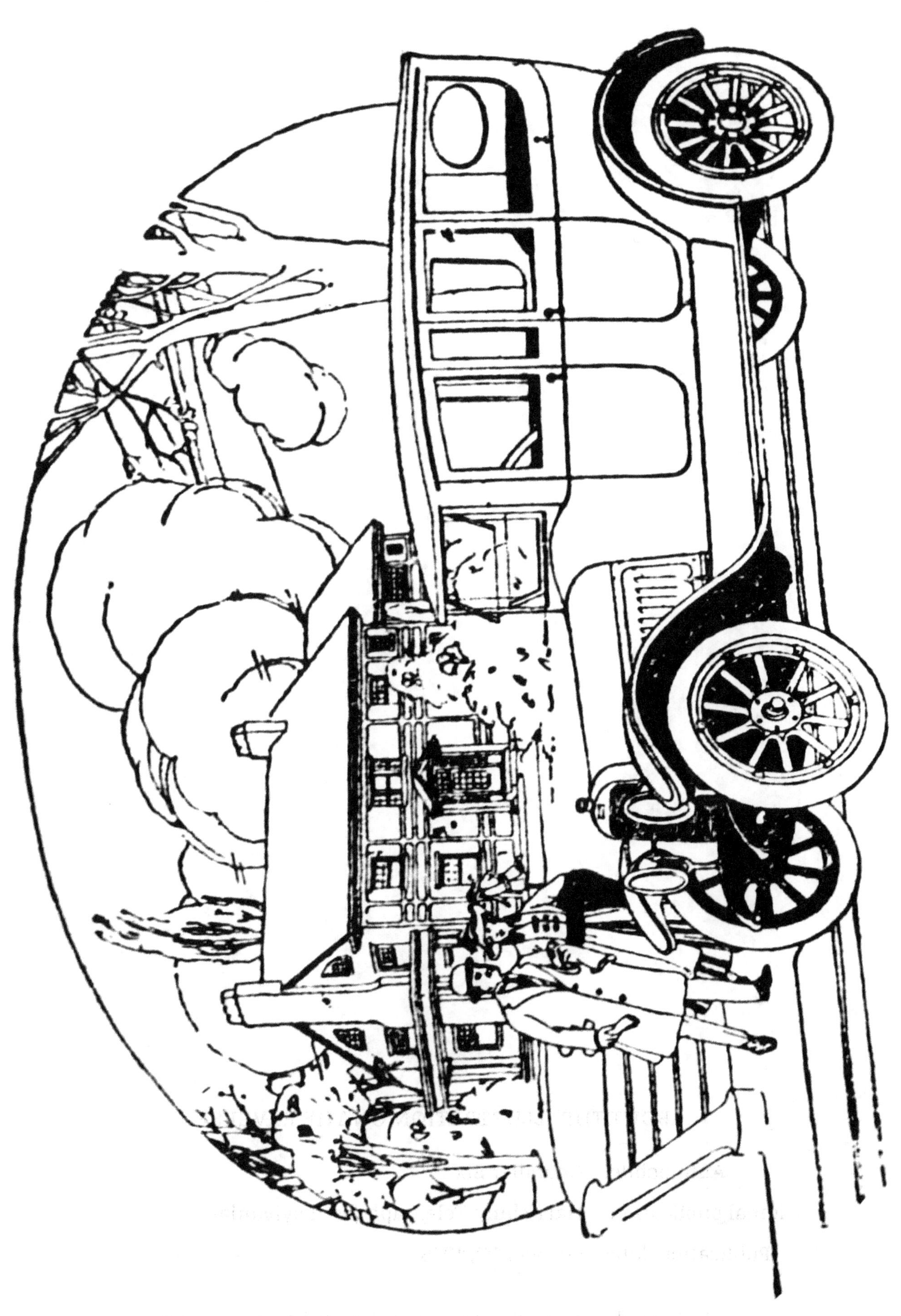

ABOUT THE ILLUSTRATION ON THE REVERSE

Automobile:	Chandler Six
Original publication:	Harrisburg Telegraph (Pennsylvania)
Publication date:	October 23, 1915

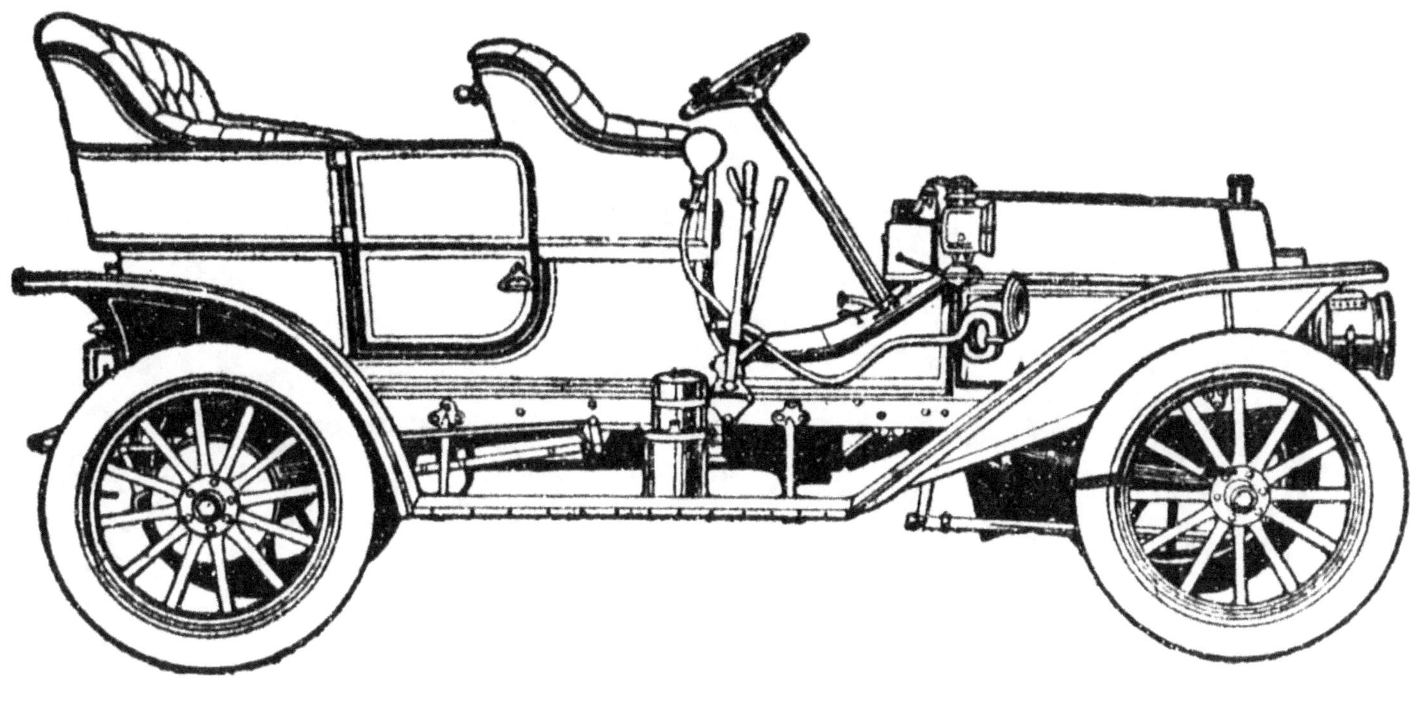

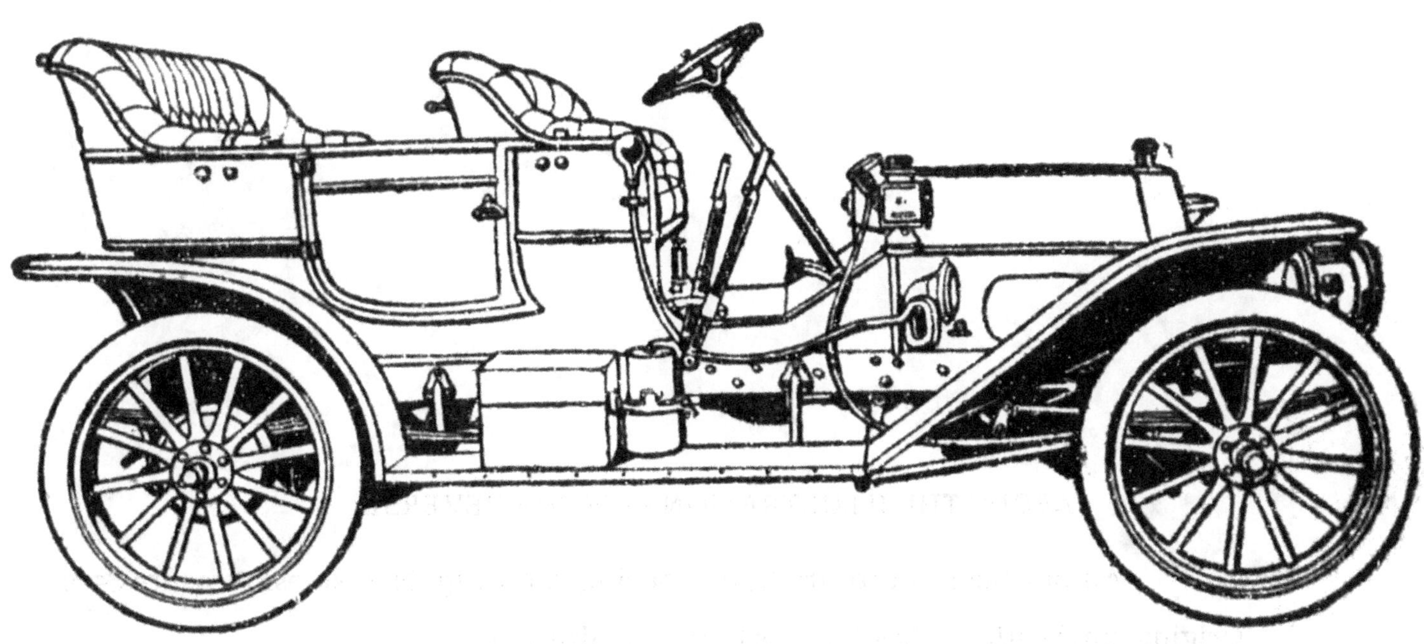

ABOUT THE ILLUSTRATIONS ON THE REVERSE

Automobile: Durocar: Type L Touring Car & Type N Business Pleasure Cars

Original publication: Los Angeles Herald (California)

Publication date: September 12, 1909

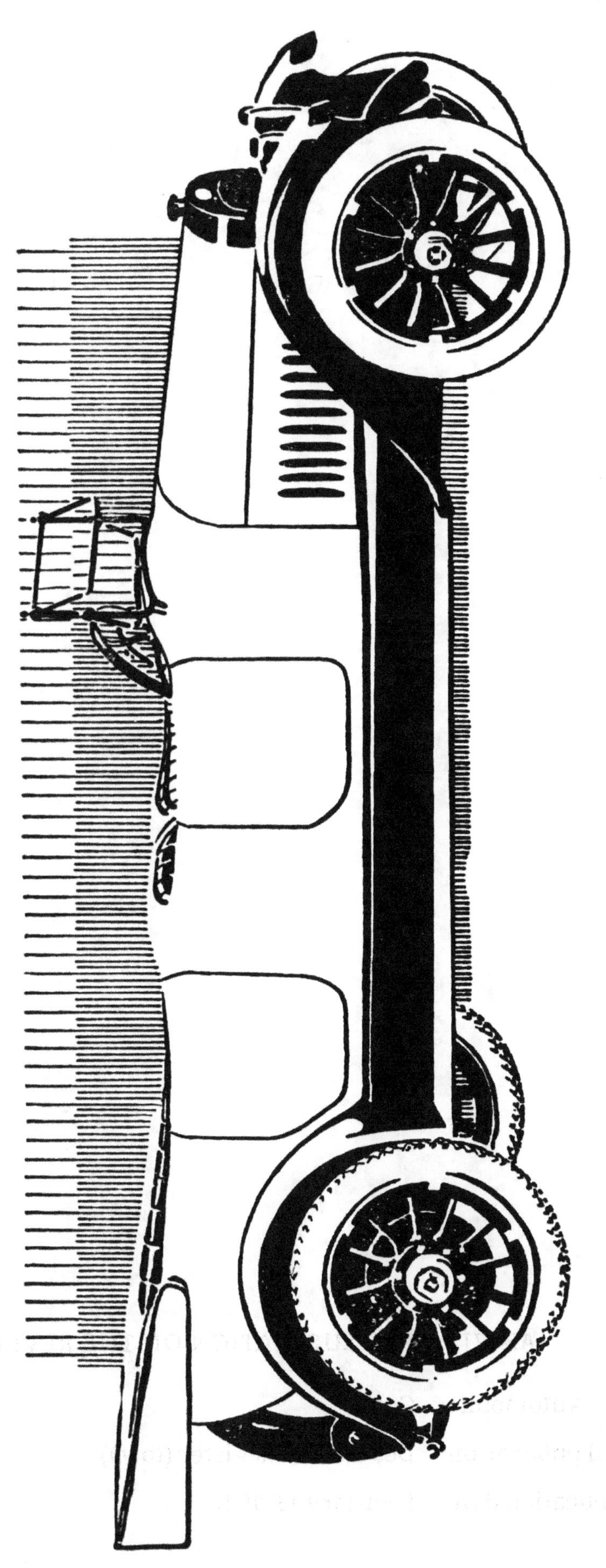

ABOUT THE ILLUSTRATION ON THE REVERSE

Automobile:	Cole 8
Original publication:	Des Moines Register (Iowa)
Publication date:	February 13, 1916

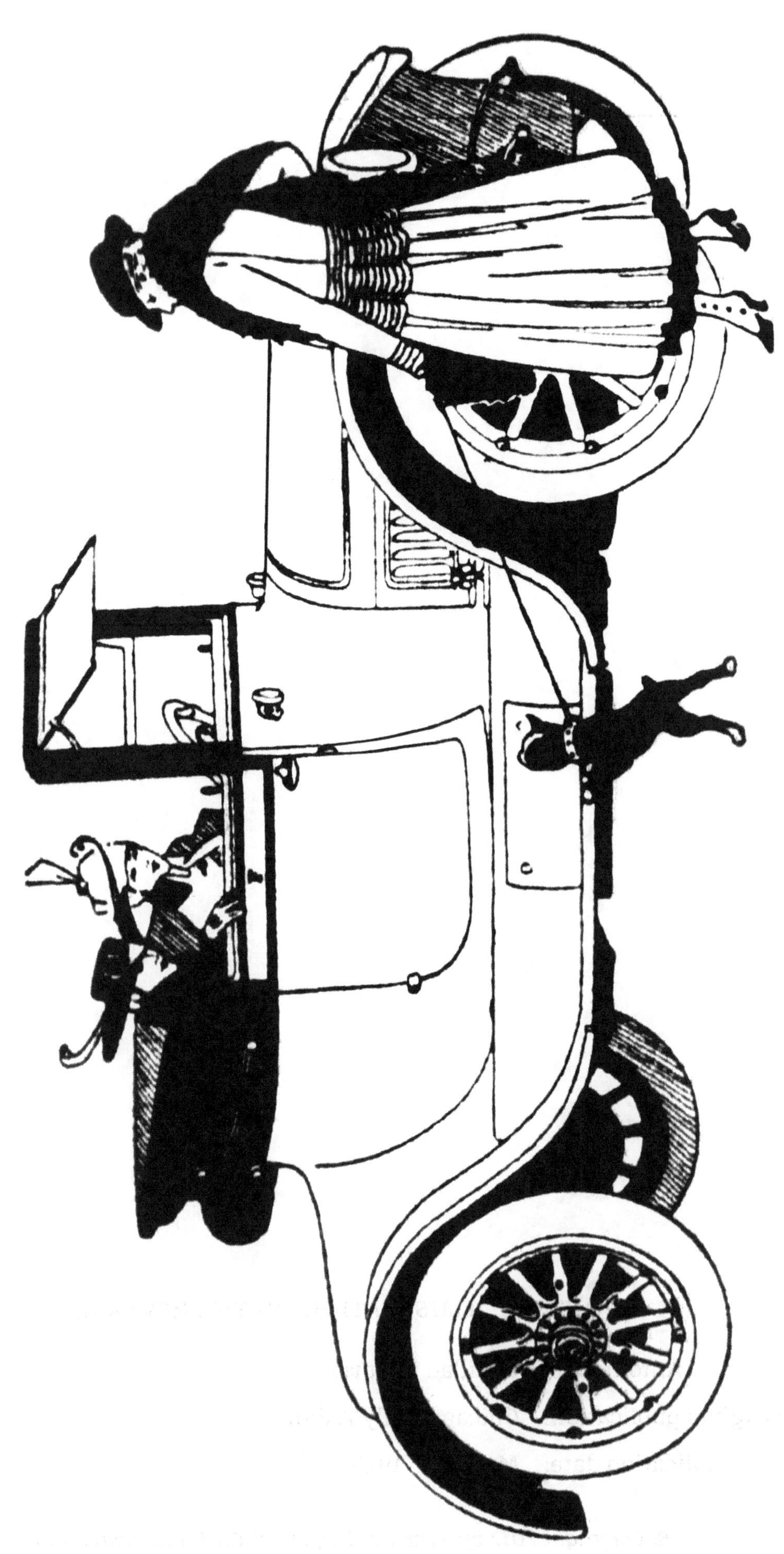

ABOUT THE ILLUSTRATION ON THE REVERSE

Automobile:	Cadillac Victoria
Original publication:	Chicago Daily Tribune
Publication date:	March 12, 1916

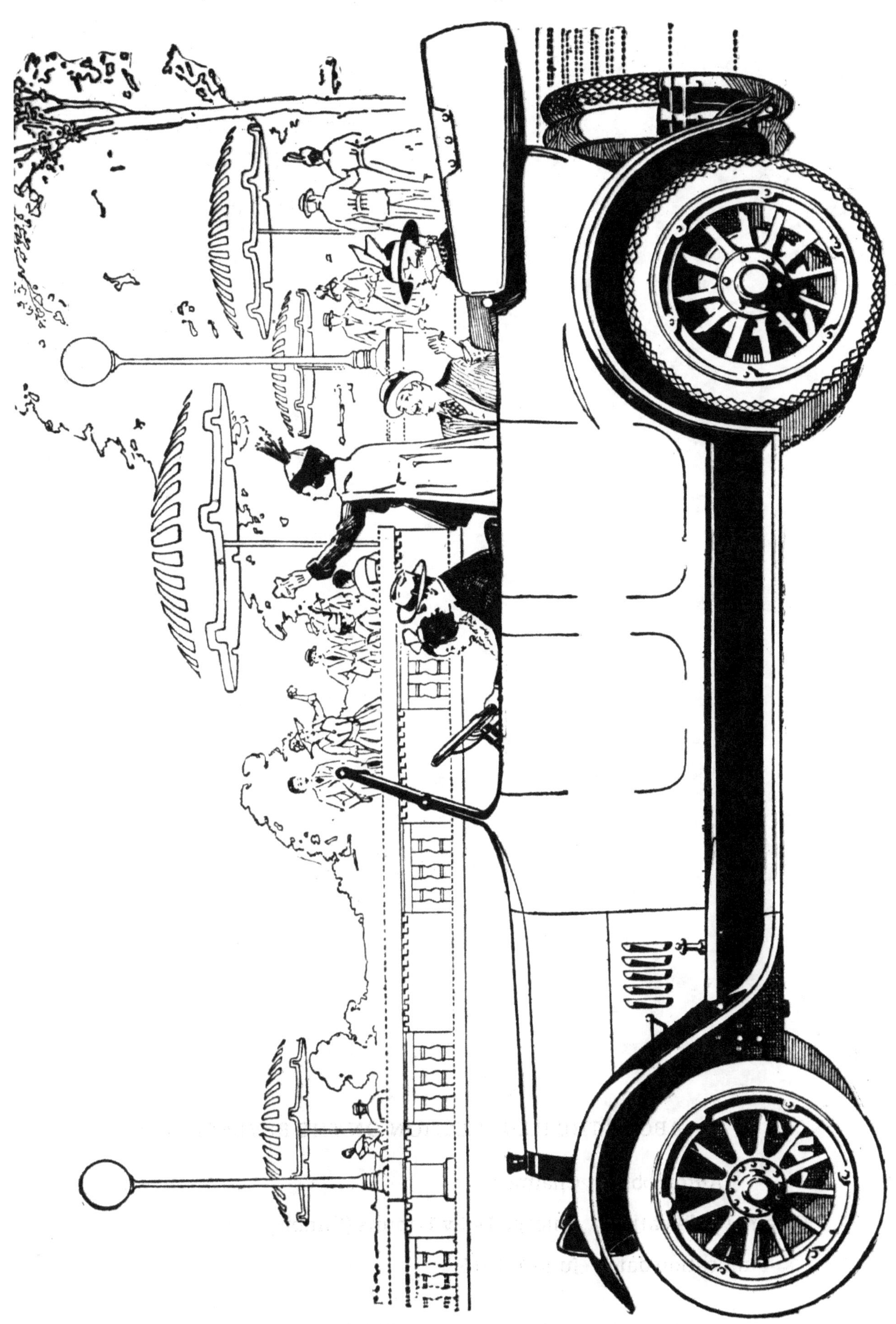

ABOUT THE ILLUSTRATION ON THE REVERSE

Automobile:	Chalmers
Original publication:	Chicago Daily Tribune (Illinois)
Publication date:	June 4, 1916

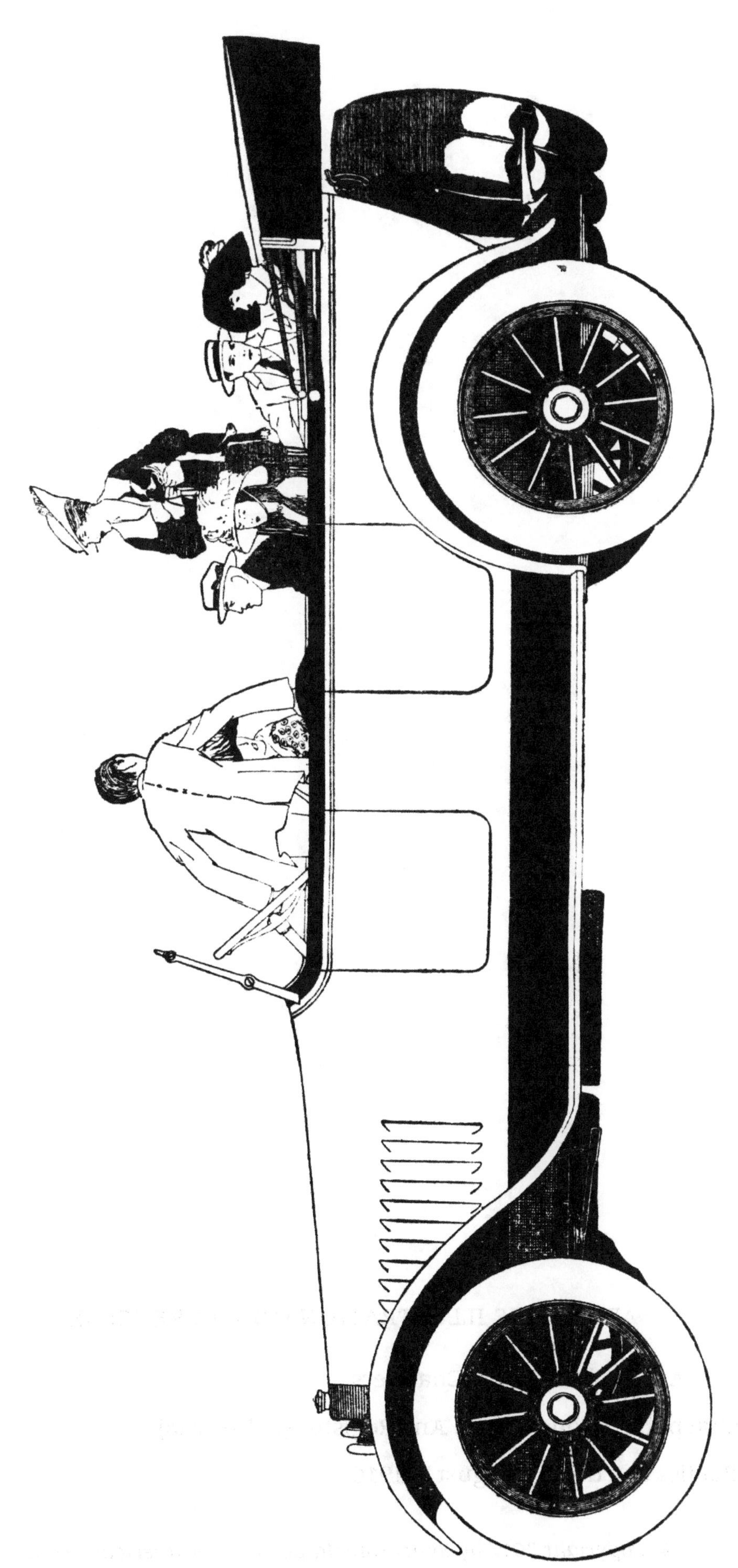

ABOUT THE ILLUSTRATION ON THE REVERSE

Automobile:	1917 Chalmers
Original publication:	Santa Ana Register (California)
Publication date:	August 3, 1916

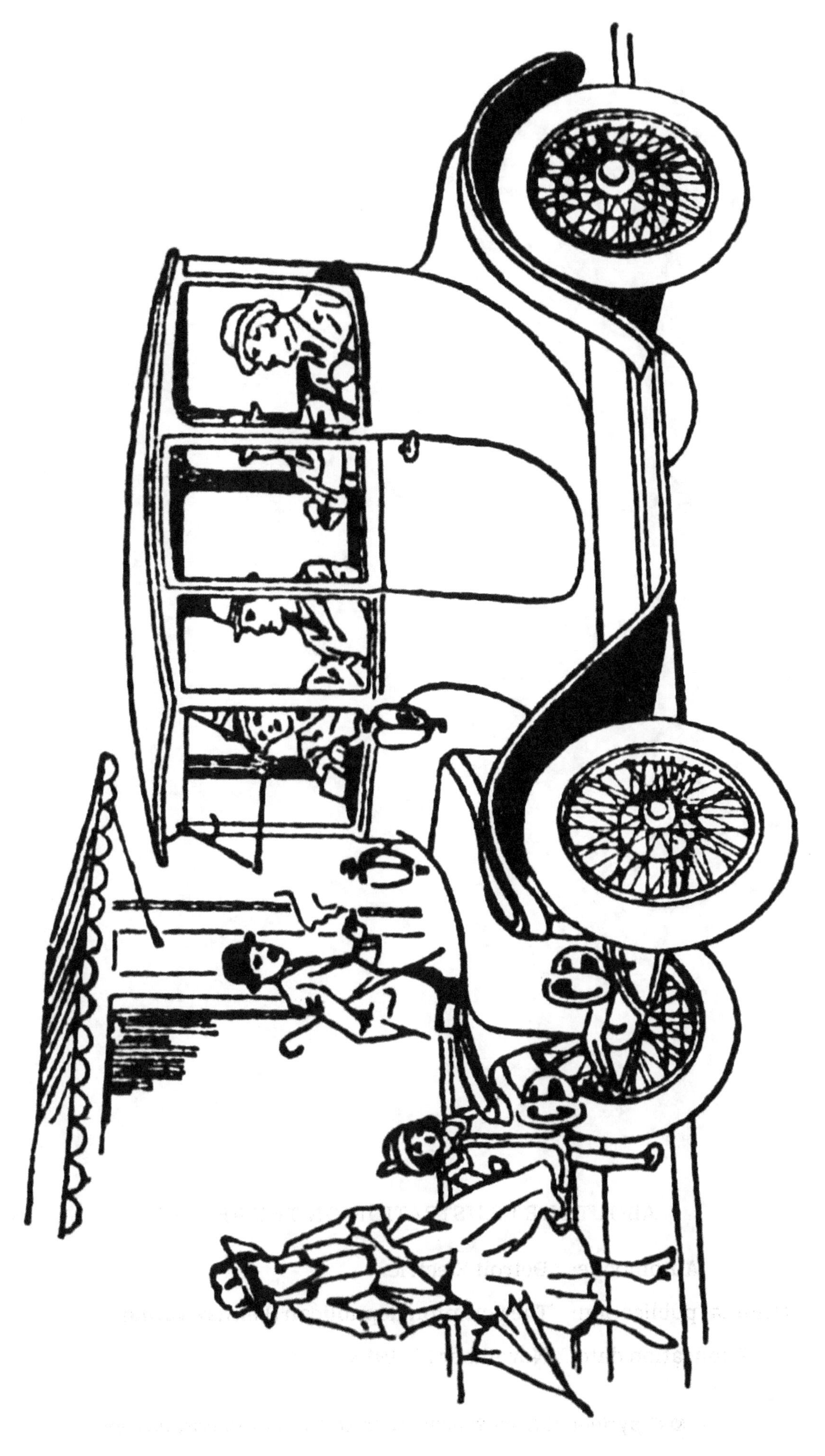

ABOUT THE ILLUSTRATION ON THE REVERSE

Automobile:	Detroit Electric
Original publication:	The Scranton Republican (Pennsylvania)
Publication date:	November 25, 1916

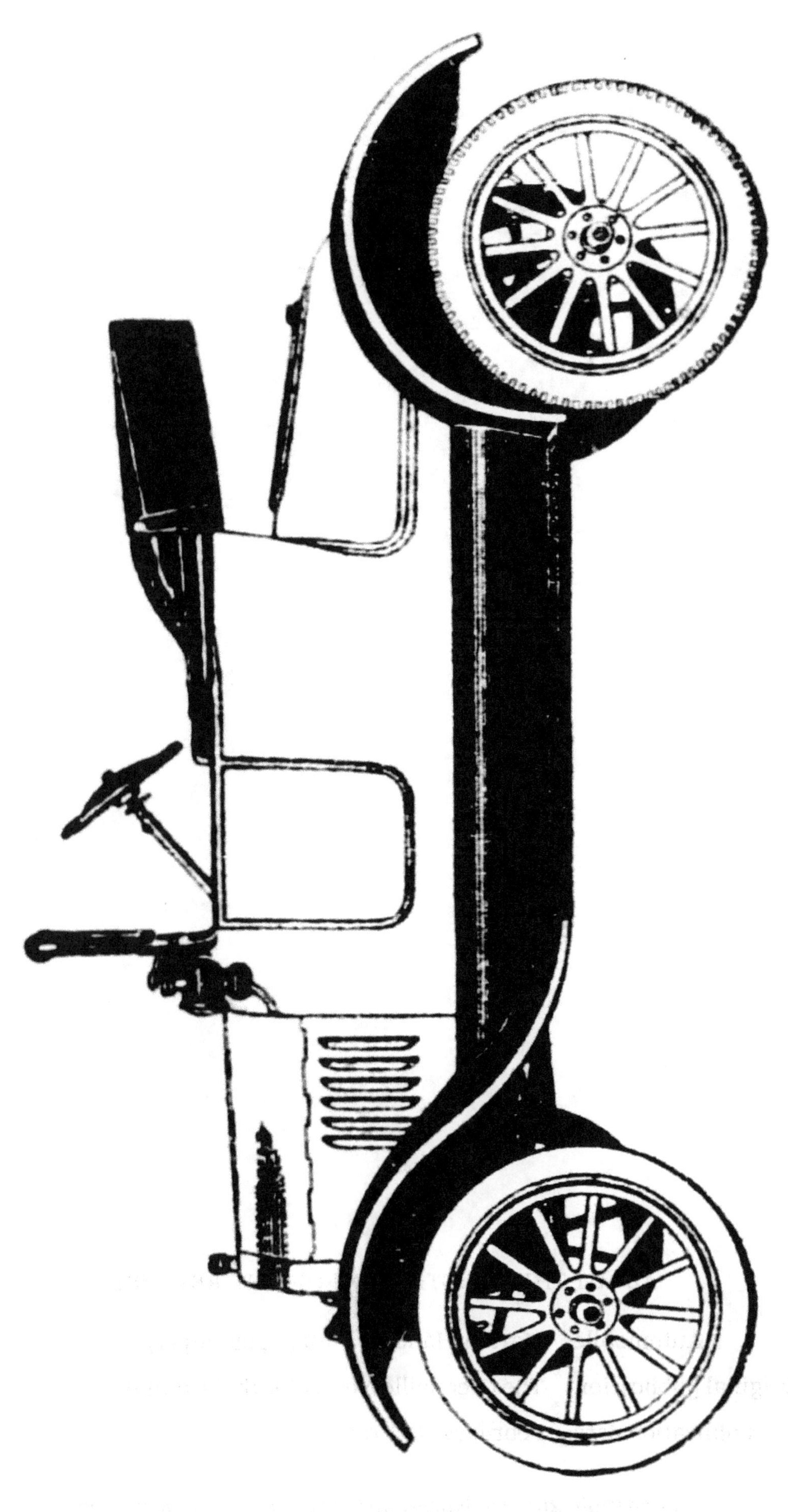

ABOUT THE ILLUSTRATION ON THE REVERSE

Automobile:	Marion-Handley 6-60 (7-passenger)
Original publication:	The Greenville News (South Carolina)
Publication date:	February 18, 1917

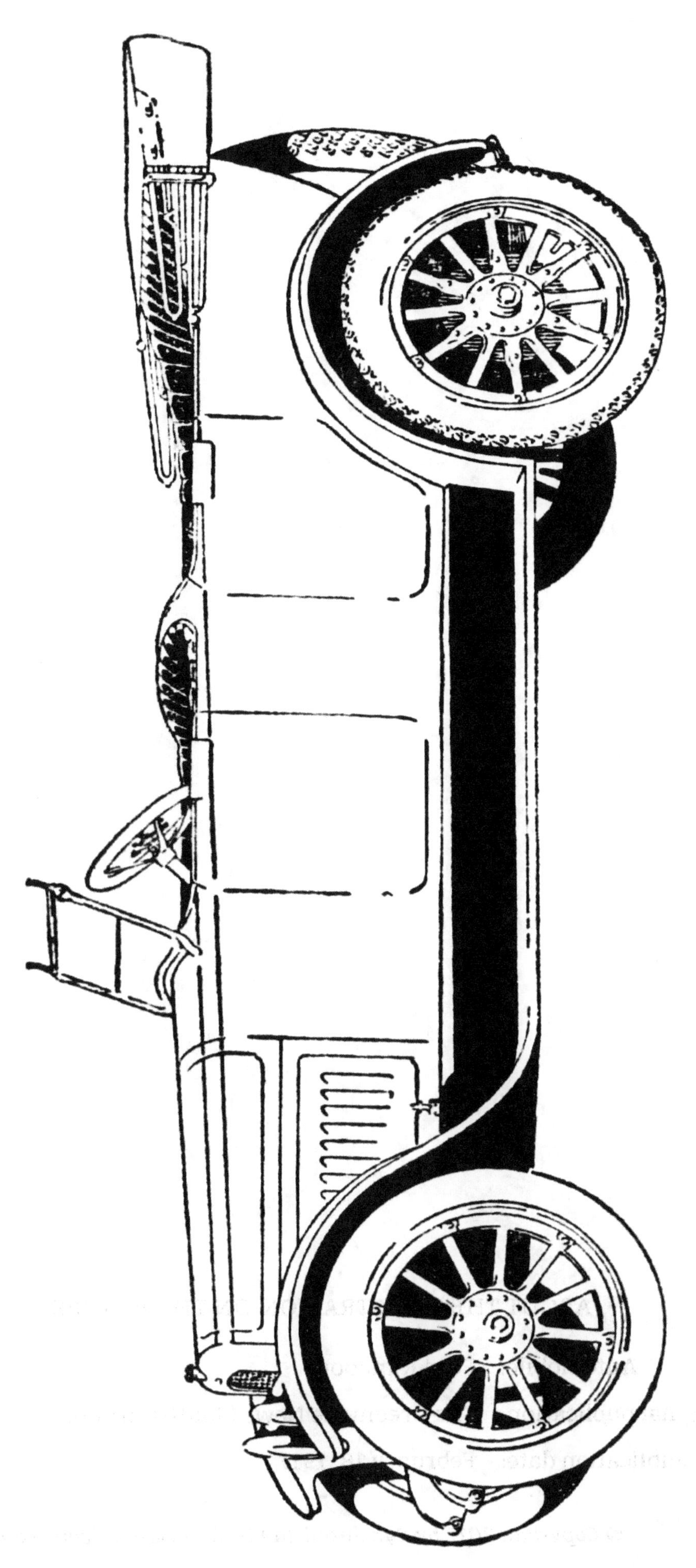

ABOUT THE ILLUSTRATION ON THE REVERSE

Automobile:	Ford Runabout
Original publication:	The Greenville News (South Carolina)
Publication date:	February 18, 1917

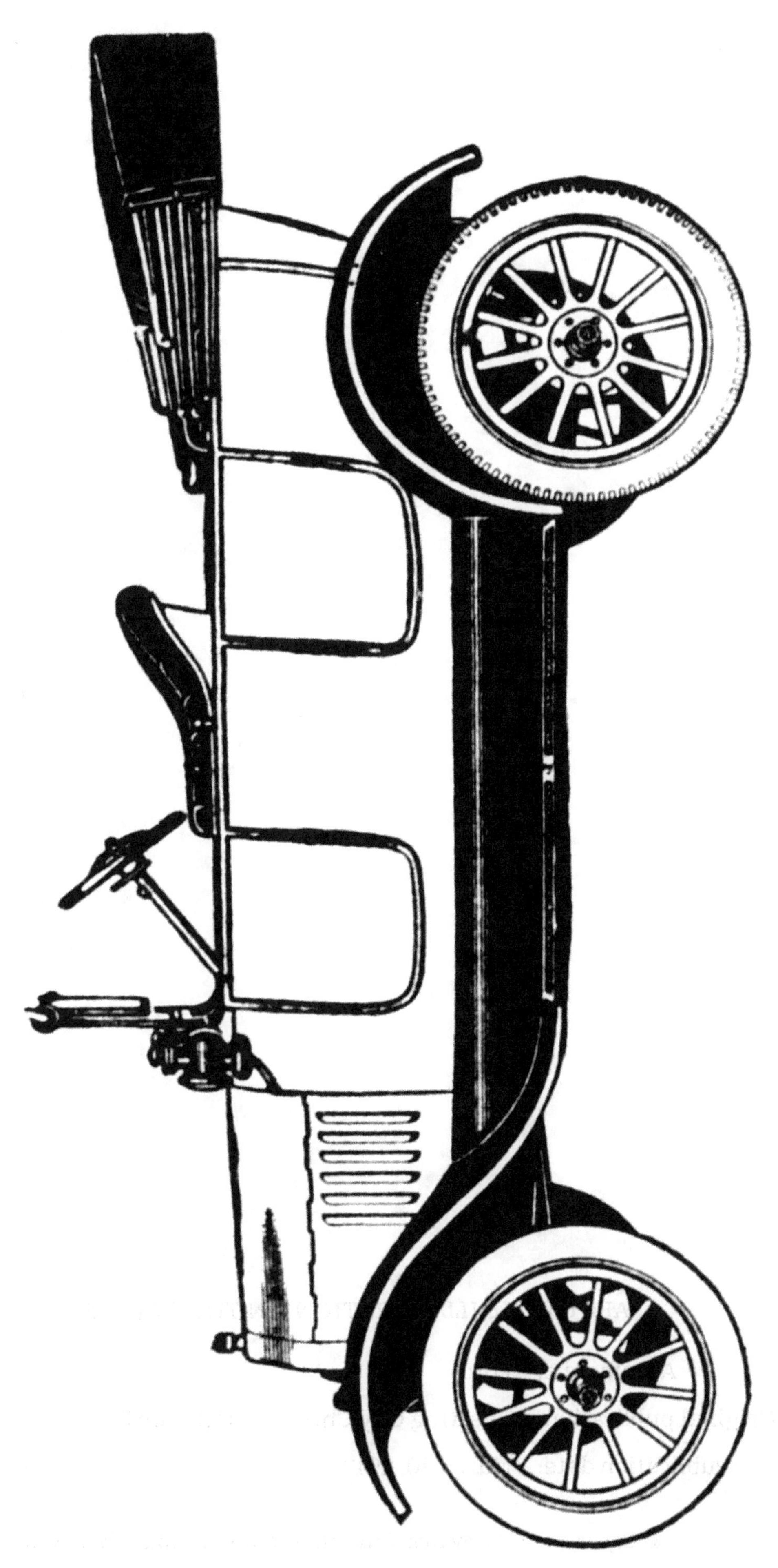

ABOUT THE ILLUSTRATION ON THE REVERSE

Automobile:	Ford
Original publication:	The King City Chronicle (Missouri)
Publication date:	March 30, 1917

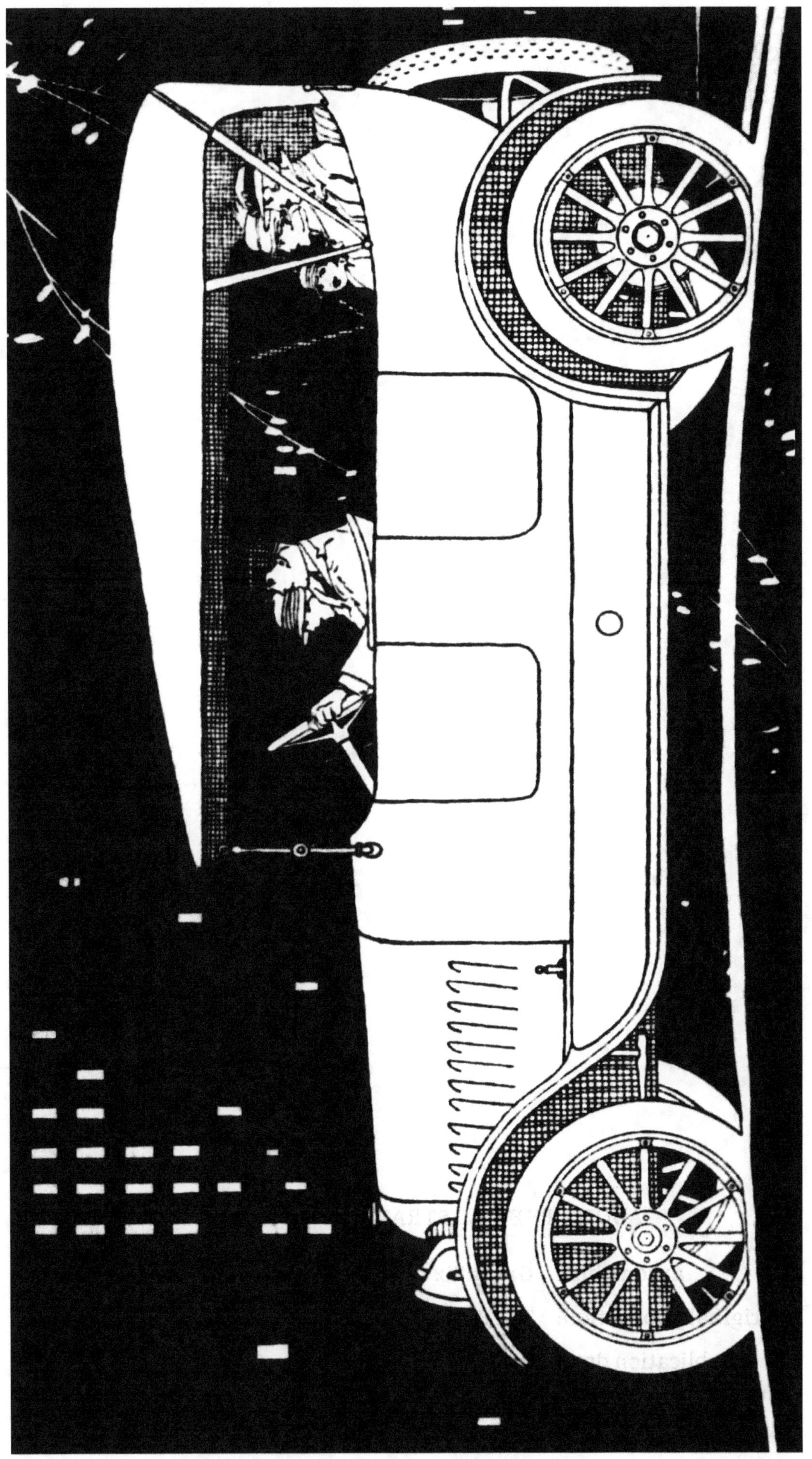

ABOUT THE ILLUSTRATION ON THE REVERSE

Automobile:	Grant Six
Original publication:	The Hood River Glacier (Oregon)
Publication date:	June 7, 1917

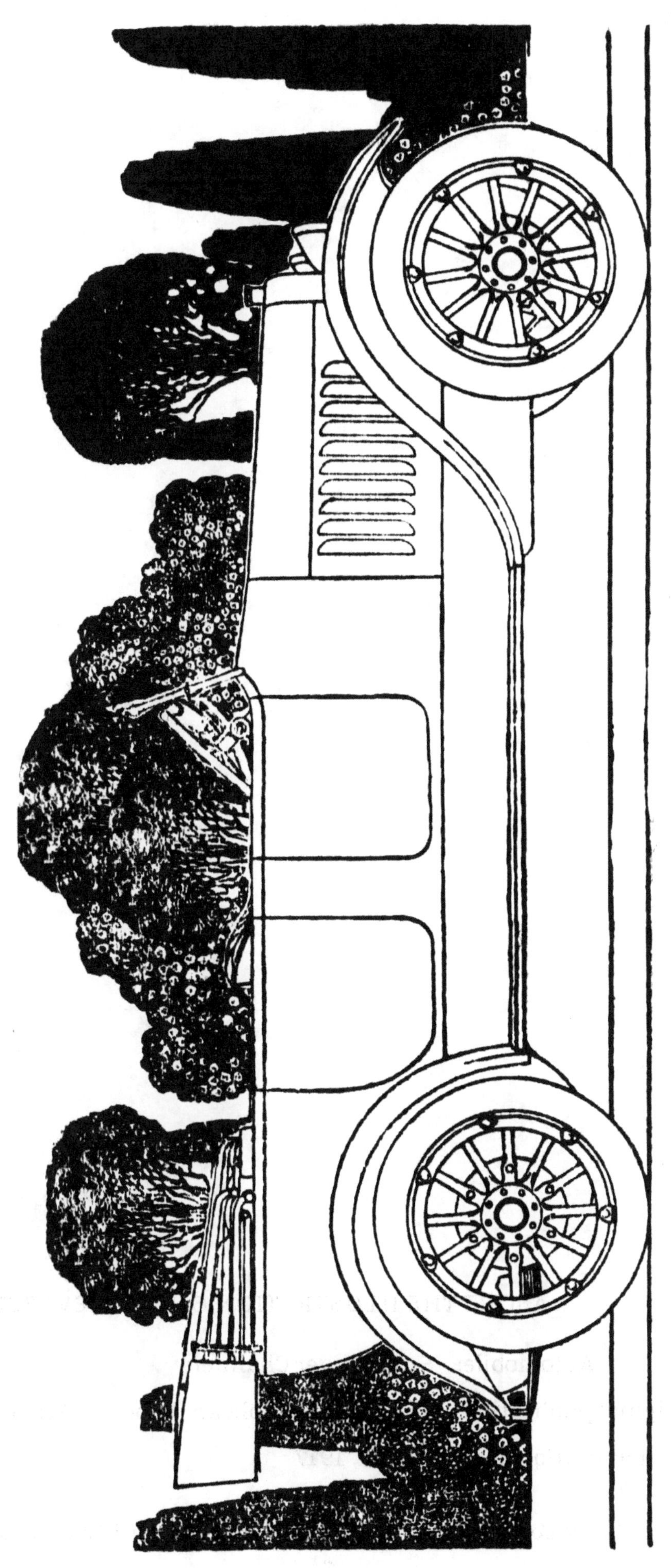

ABOUT THE ILLUSTRATION ON THE REVERSE

Automobile:	5-passenger Chalmers
Original publication:	The Daily Republican (Phoenix, Arizona)
Publication date:	July 31, 1917

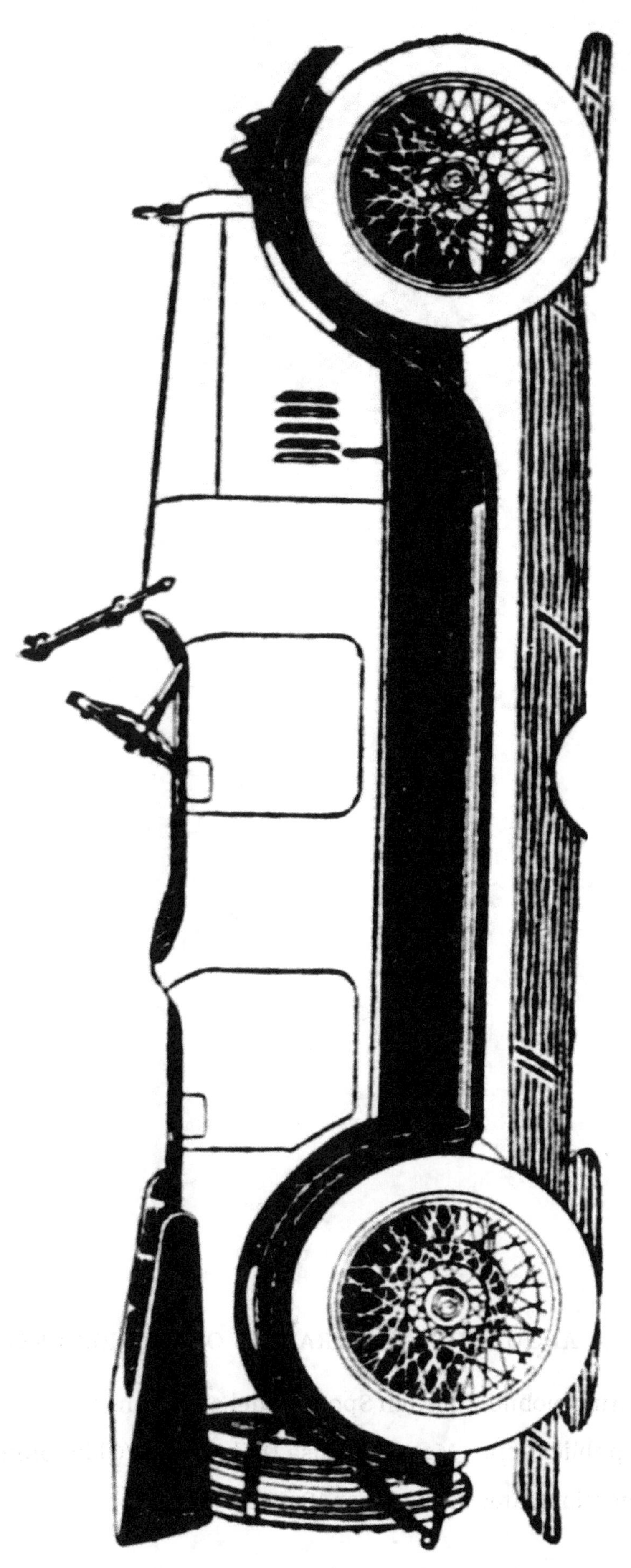

ABOUT THE ILLUSTRATION ON THE REVERSE

Automobile:	Jordan Sport Model 4-passenger
Original publication:	Morning Tulsa Daily World (Oklahoma)
Publication date:	November 18, 1917

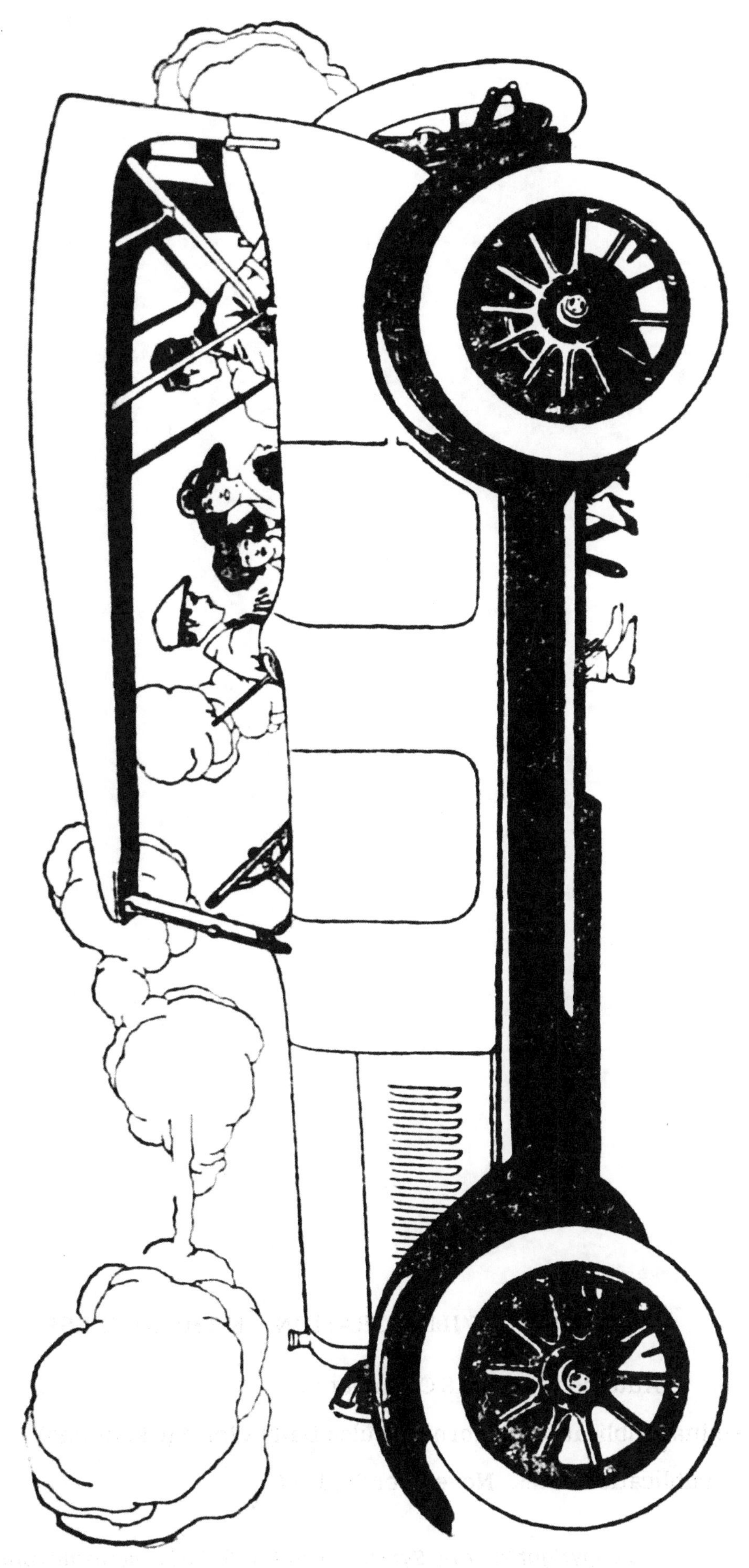

ABOUT THE ILLUSTRATION ON THE REVERSE

Automobile: 1918 Chandler Six

Original publication: Morning Tulsa Daily World (Oklahoma)

Publication date: November 25, 1917

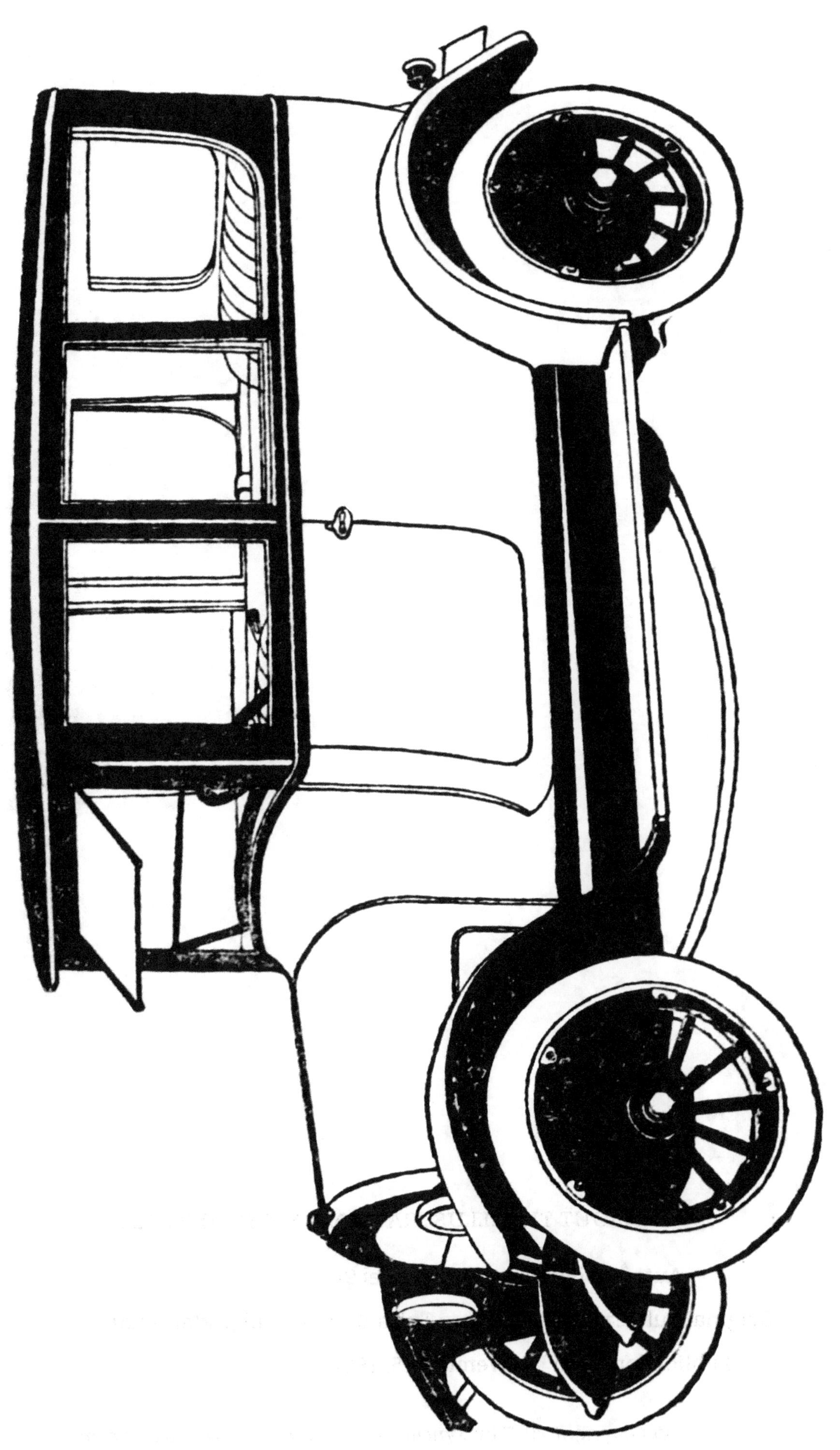

ABOUT THE ILLUSTRATION ON THE REVERSE

Automobile:	Overland Model 90
Original publication:	Morning Tulsa Daily World (Oklahoma)
Publication date:	November 25, 1917

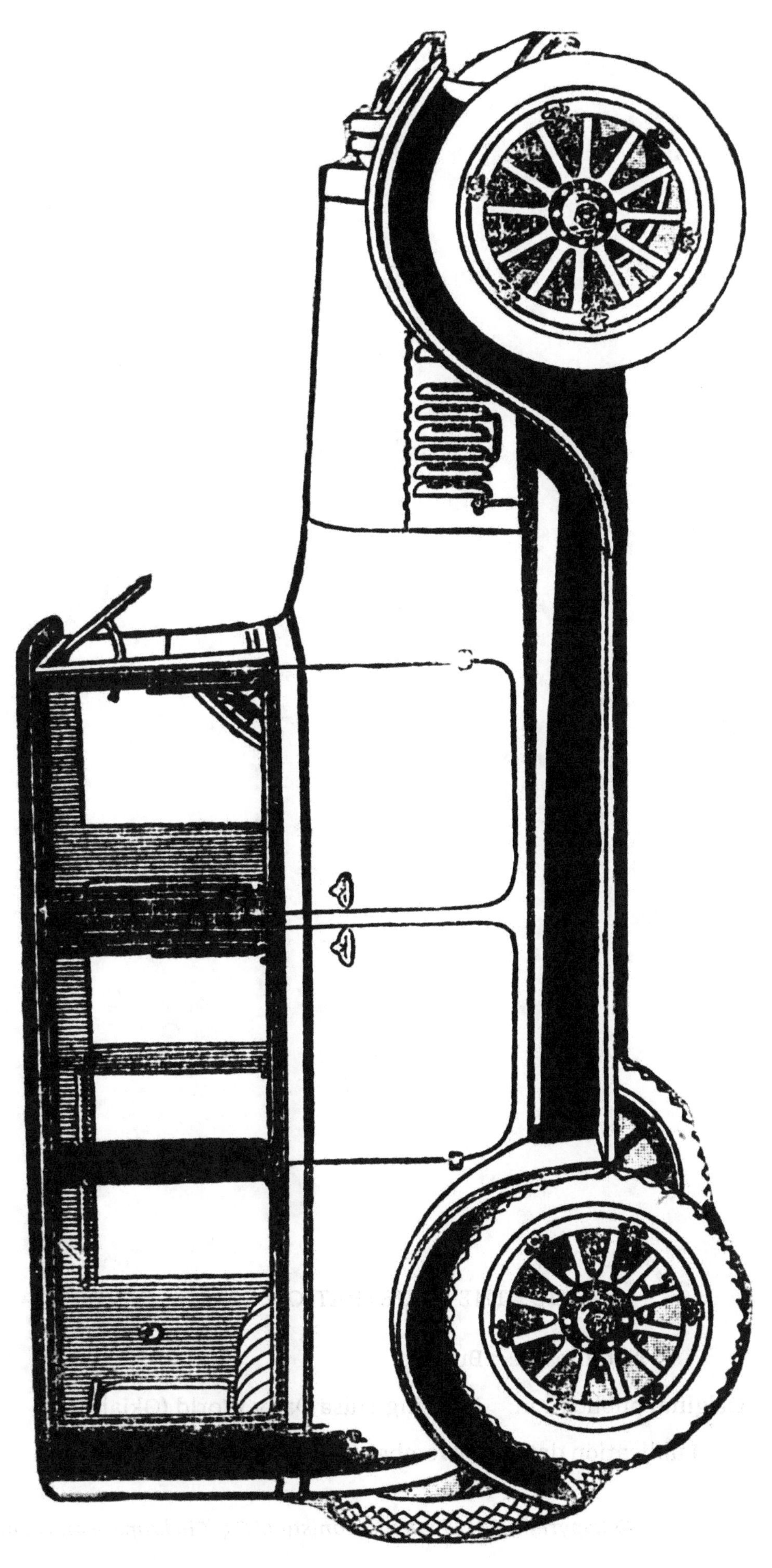

ABOUT THE ILLUSTRATION ON THE REVERSE

Automobile:	Buick
Original publication:	Morning Tulsa Daily World (Oklahoma)
Publication date:	November 25, 1917

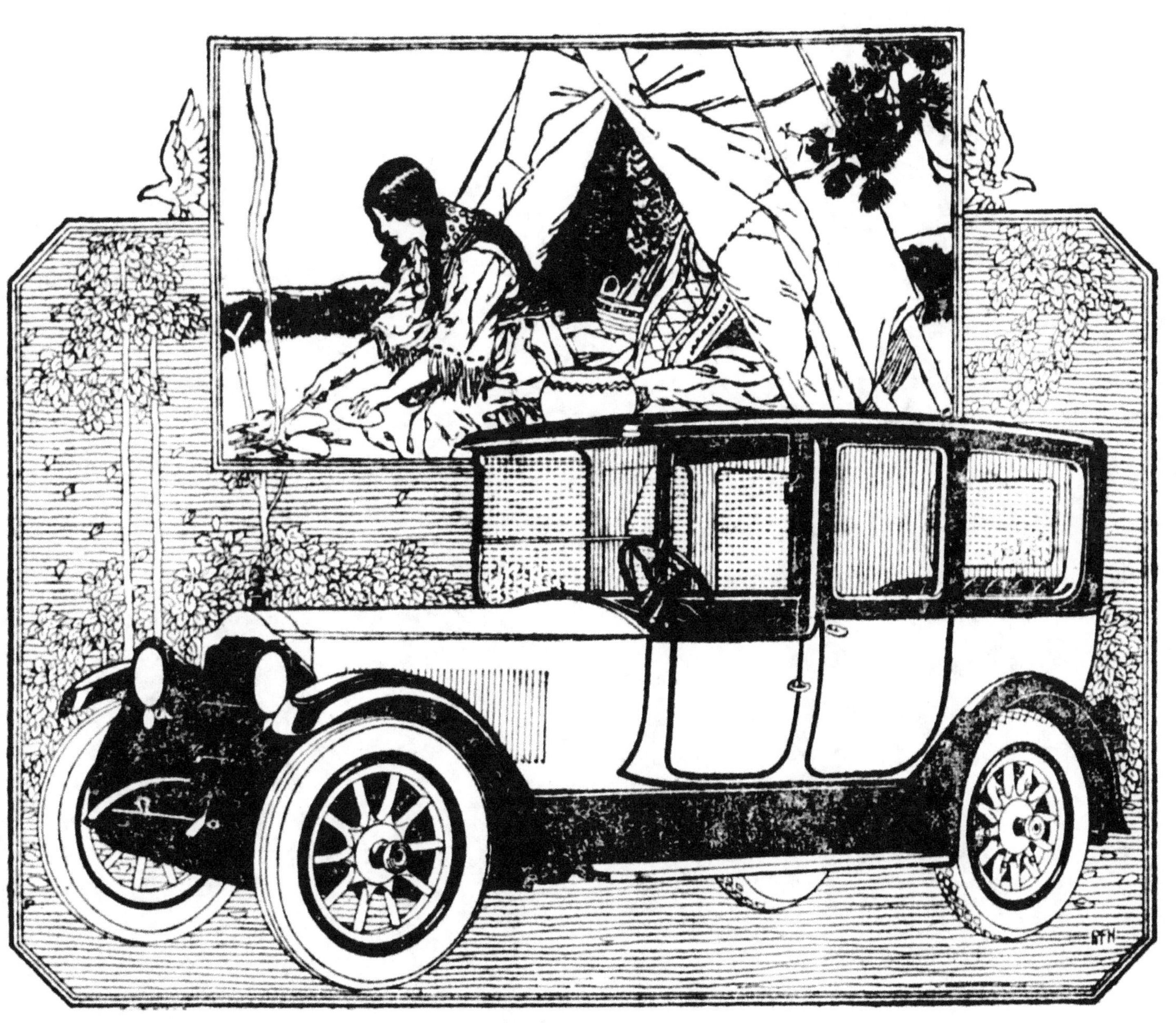

ABOUT THE ILLUSTRATION ON THE REVERSE

Automobile:	Packard Limousine
Original publication:	Morning Tulsa Daily World (Oklahoma)
Publication date:	November 25, 1917

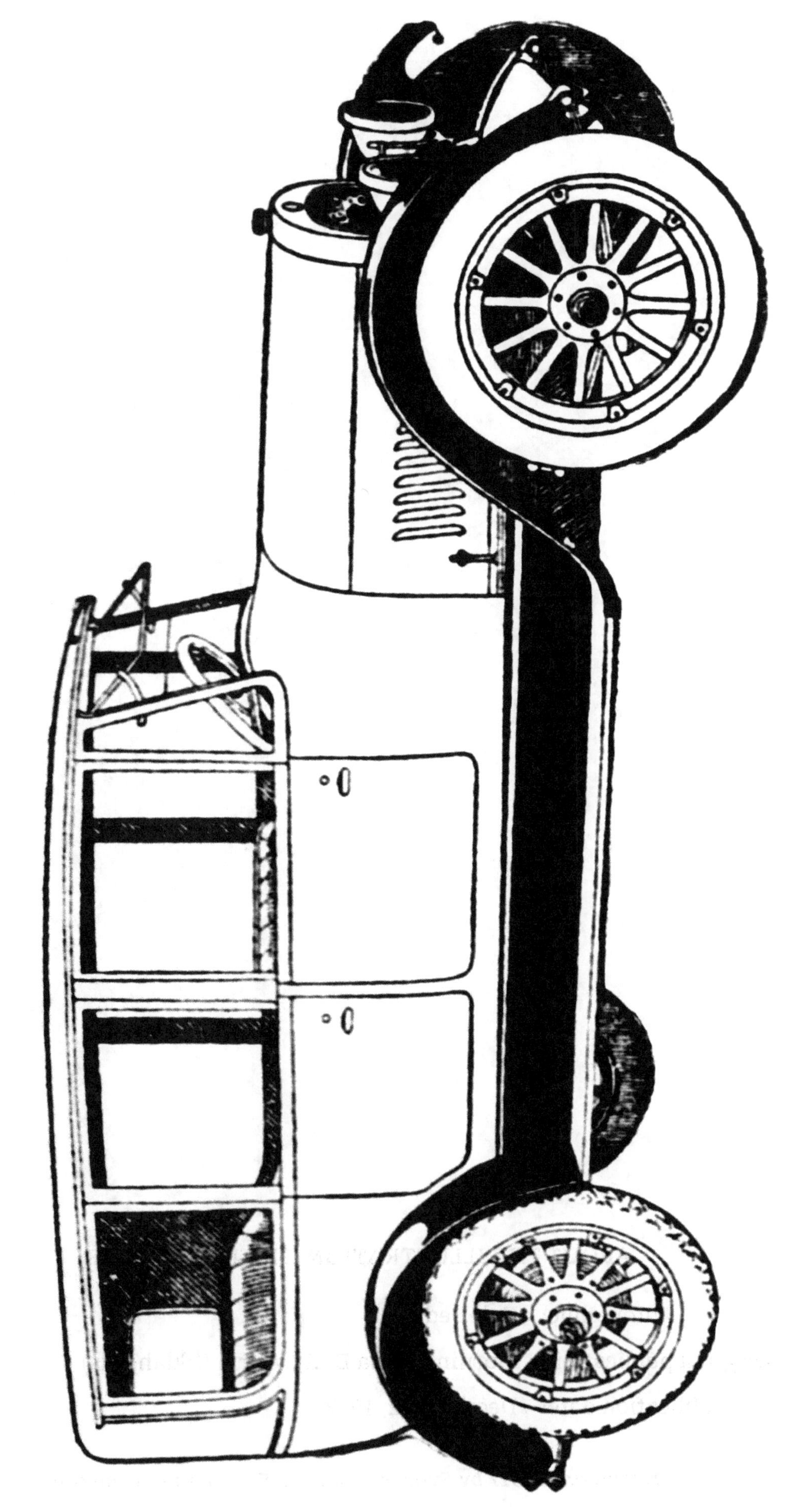

ABOUT THE ILLUSTRATION ON THE REVERSE

Automobile: Cole Sedan

Original publication: Morning Tulsa Daily World (Oklahoma)

Publication date: December 2, 1917

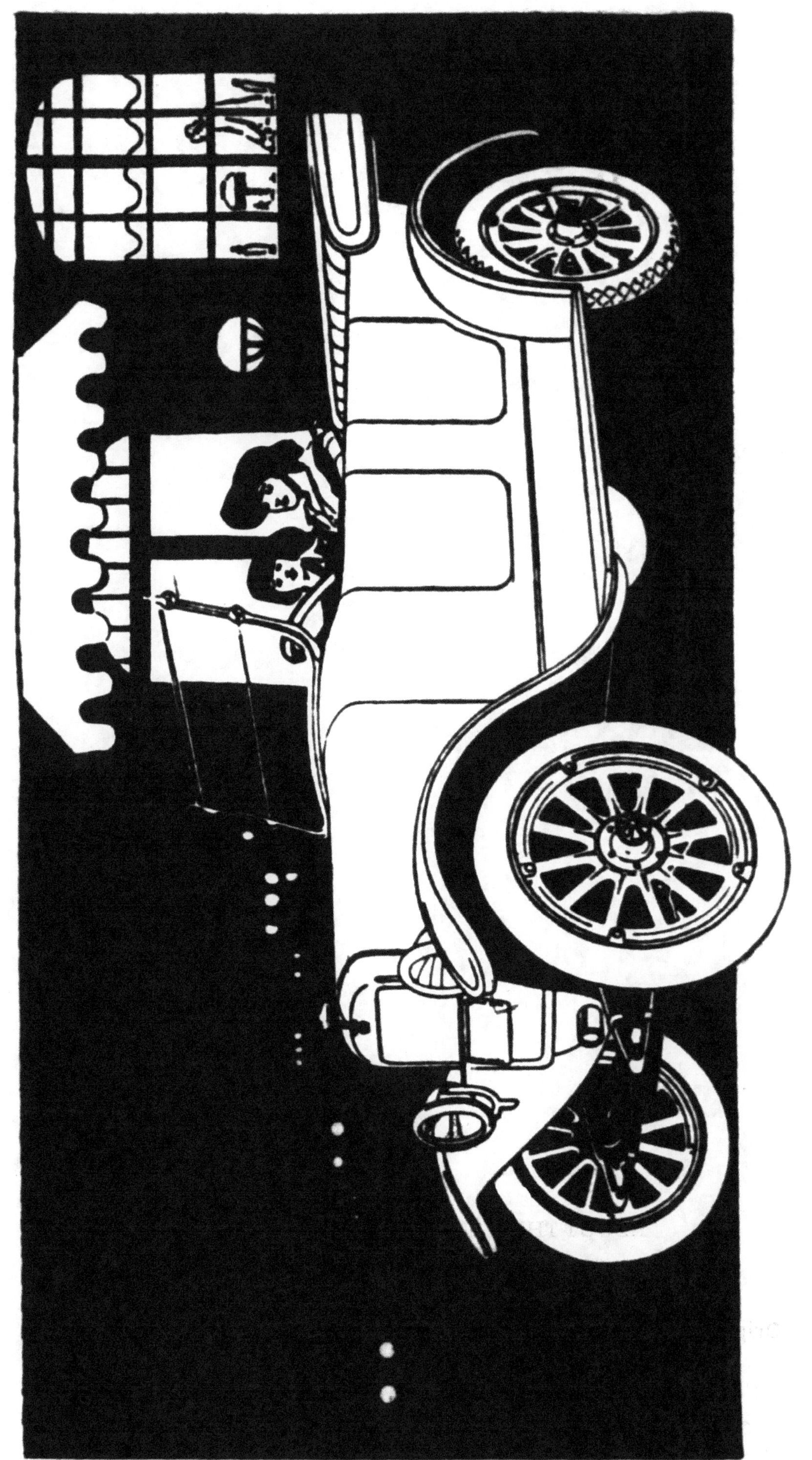

ABOUT THE ILLUSTRATION ON THE REVERSE

Automobile: Briscoe

Original publication: San Francisco Chronicle (California)

Publication date: December 23, 1917

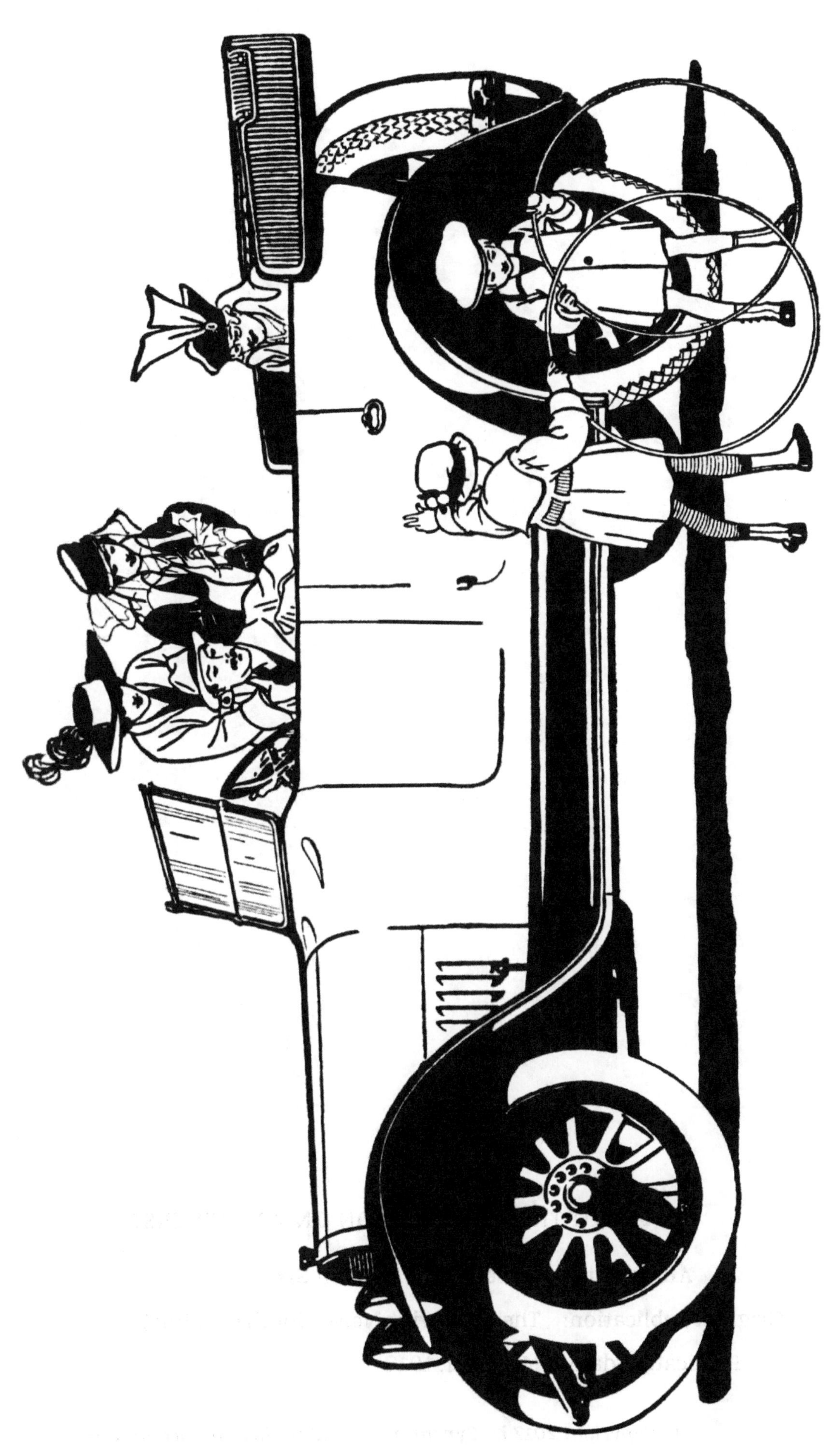

ABOUT THE ILLUSTRATION ON THE REVERSE

Automobile:	Kissel Hundred Point Six
Original publication:	The Greenville News (South Carolina)
Publication date:	March 31, 1918

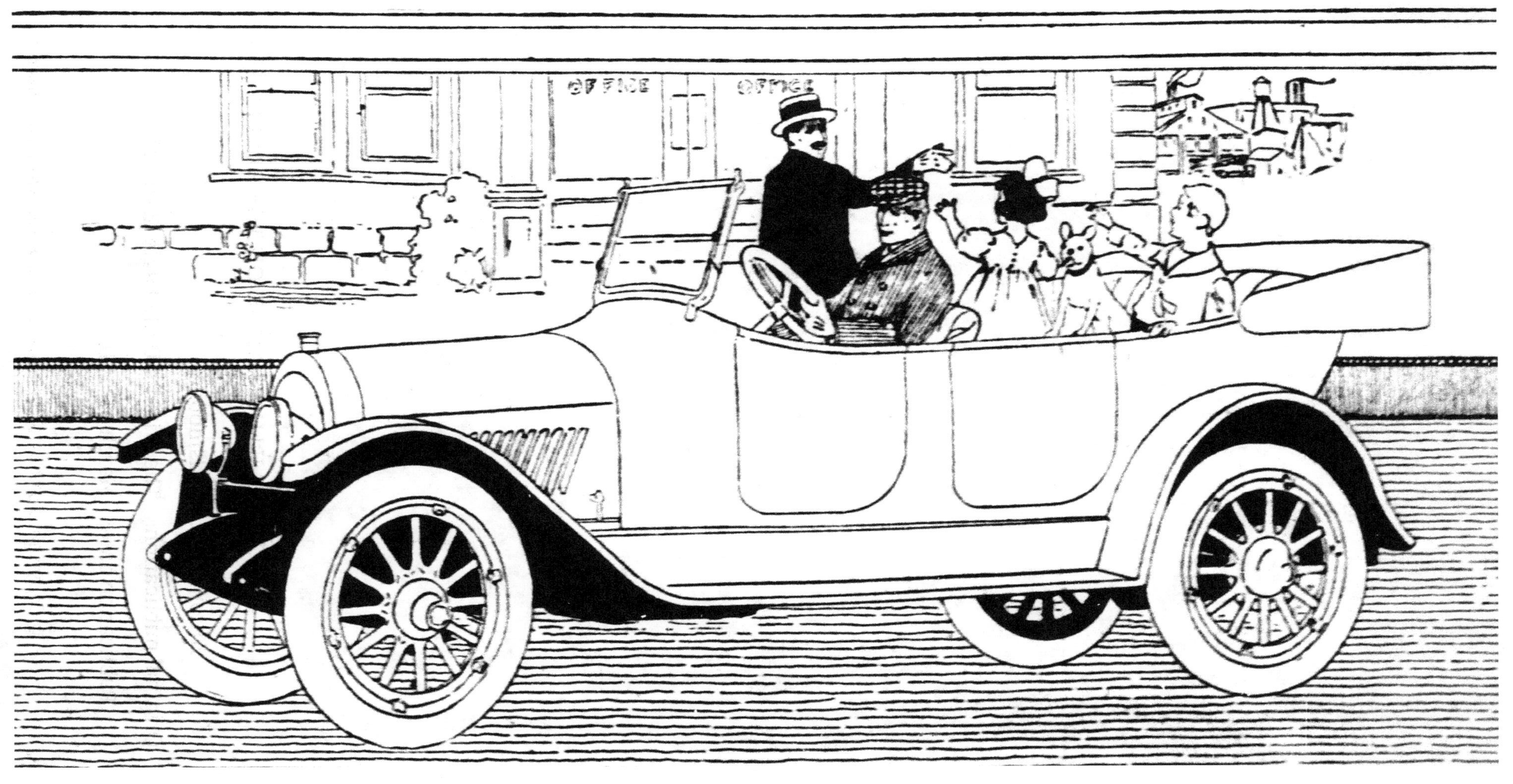
OFFICE
OFFICE

ABOUT THE ILLUSTRATION ON THE REVERSE

Automobile:	Oldsmobile
Original publication:	The Wichita Daily Eagle (Kansas)
Publication date:	March 31, 1918

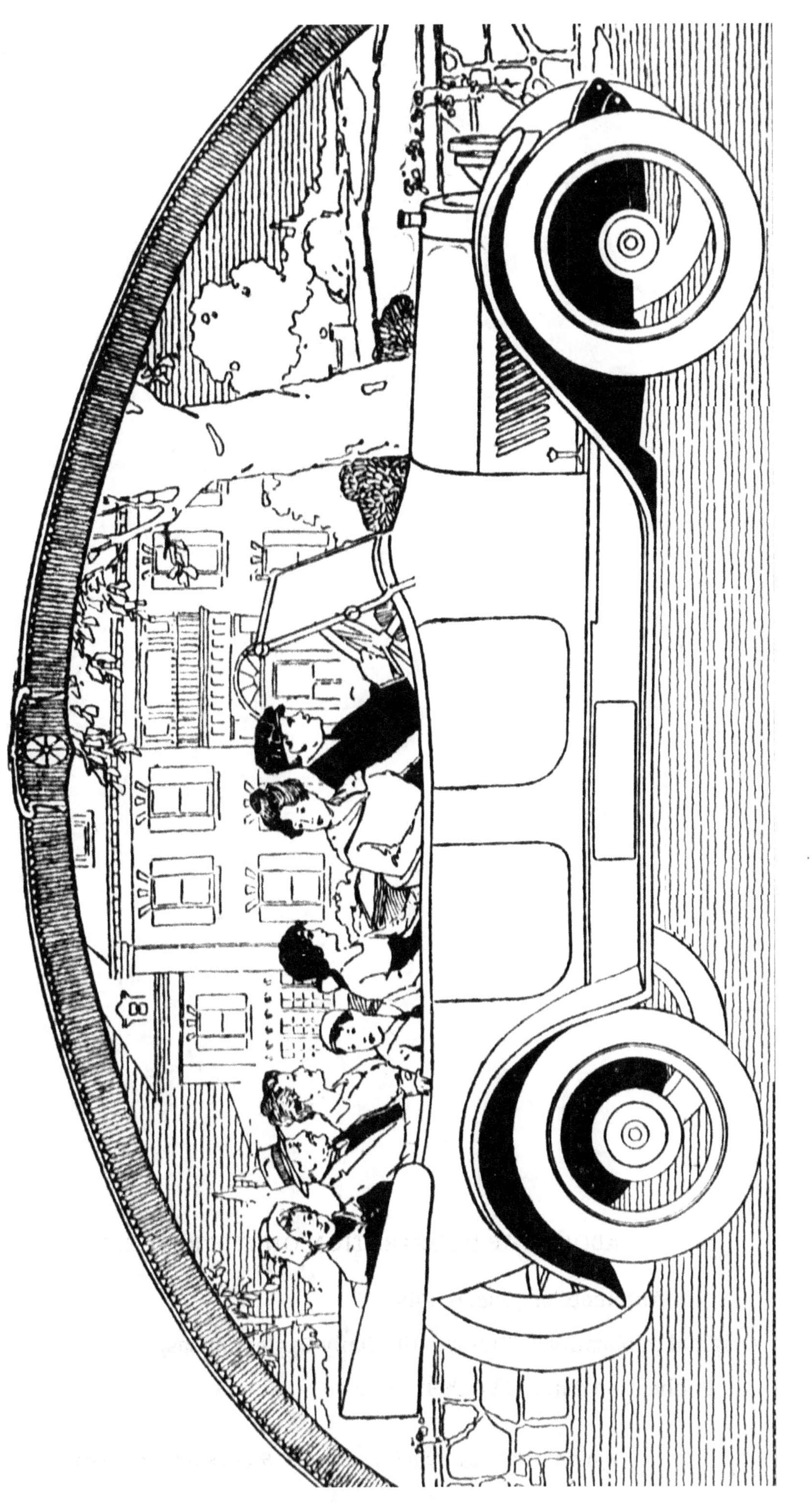

ABOUT THE ILLUSTRATION ON THE REVERSE

Automobile:	Oldsmobile
Original publication:	The Wichita Daily Eagle (Kansas)
Publication date:	March 31, 1918

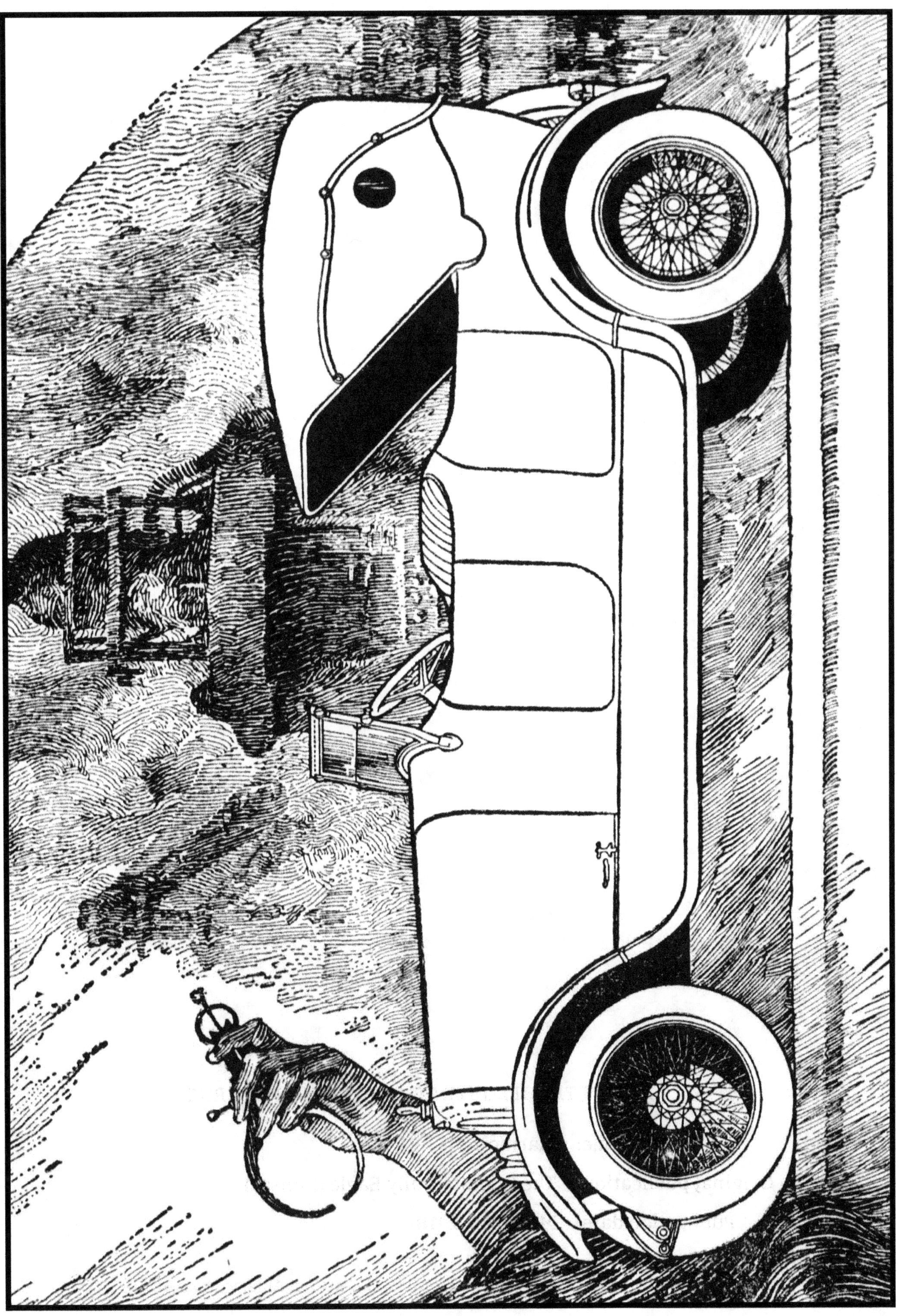

ABOUT THE ILLUSTRATION ON THE REVERSE

Automobile:	Marmon 34
Original publication:	The Wichita Daily Eagle (Kansas)
Publication date:	March 31, 1918

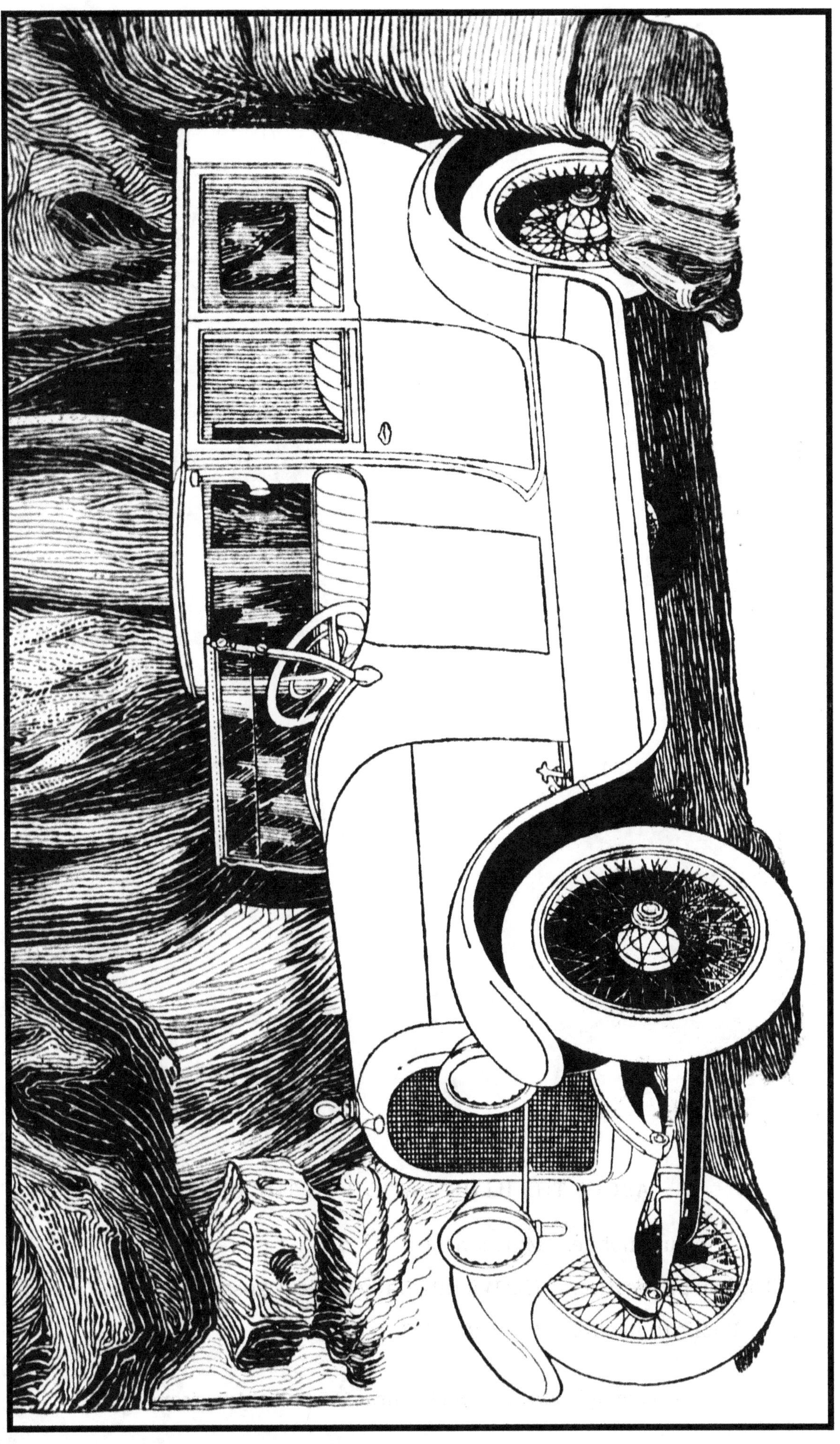

ABOUT THE ILLUSTRATION ON THE REVERSE

Automobile:	Marmon 34
Original publication:	The Wichita Daily Eagle (Kansas)
Publication date:	April 20, 1918

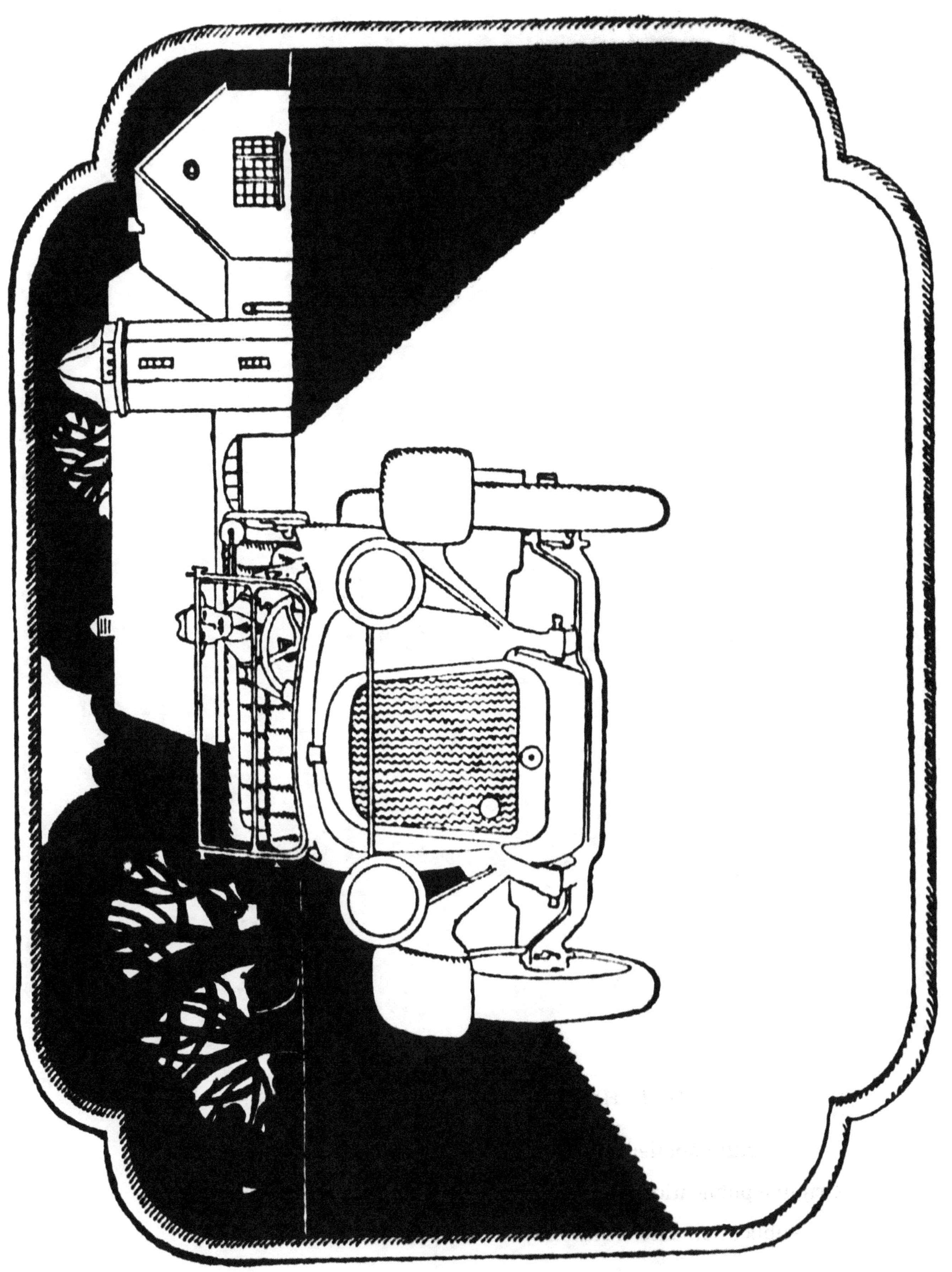

ABOUT THE ILLUSTRATION ON THE REVERSE

Automobile: Chalmers

Original publication: The Philadelphia Inquirer (Pennsylvania)

Publication date: March 9, 1919

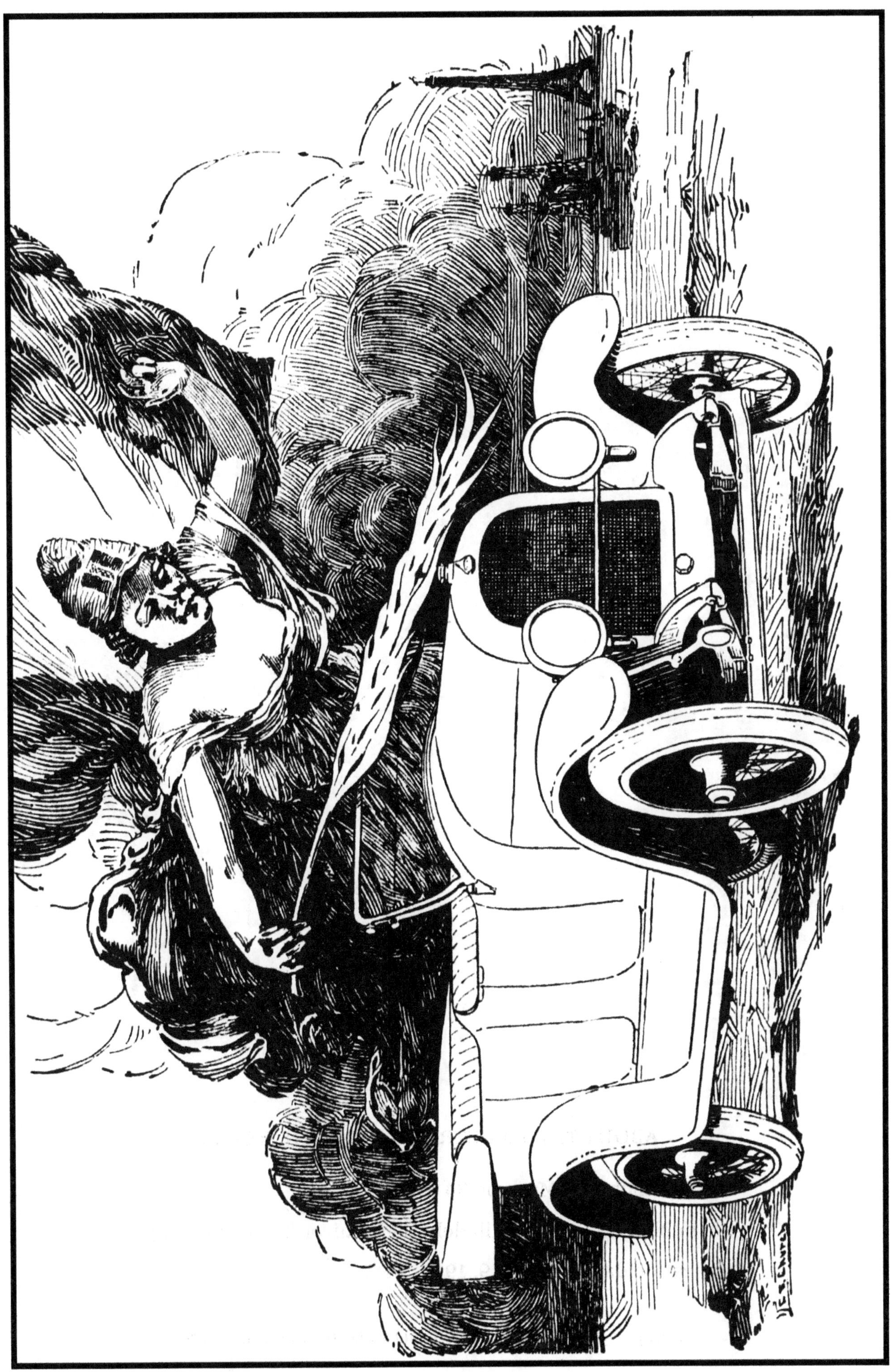

ABOUT THE ILLUSTRATION ON THE REVERSE

Automobile: Marmon 34

Original publication: The Philadelphia Inquirer (Pennsylvania)

Publication date: March 9, 1919

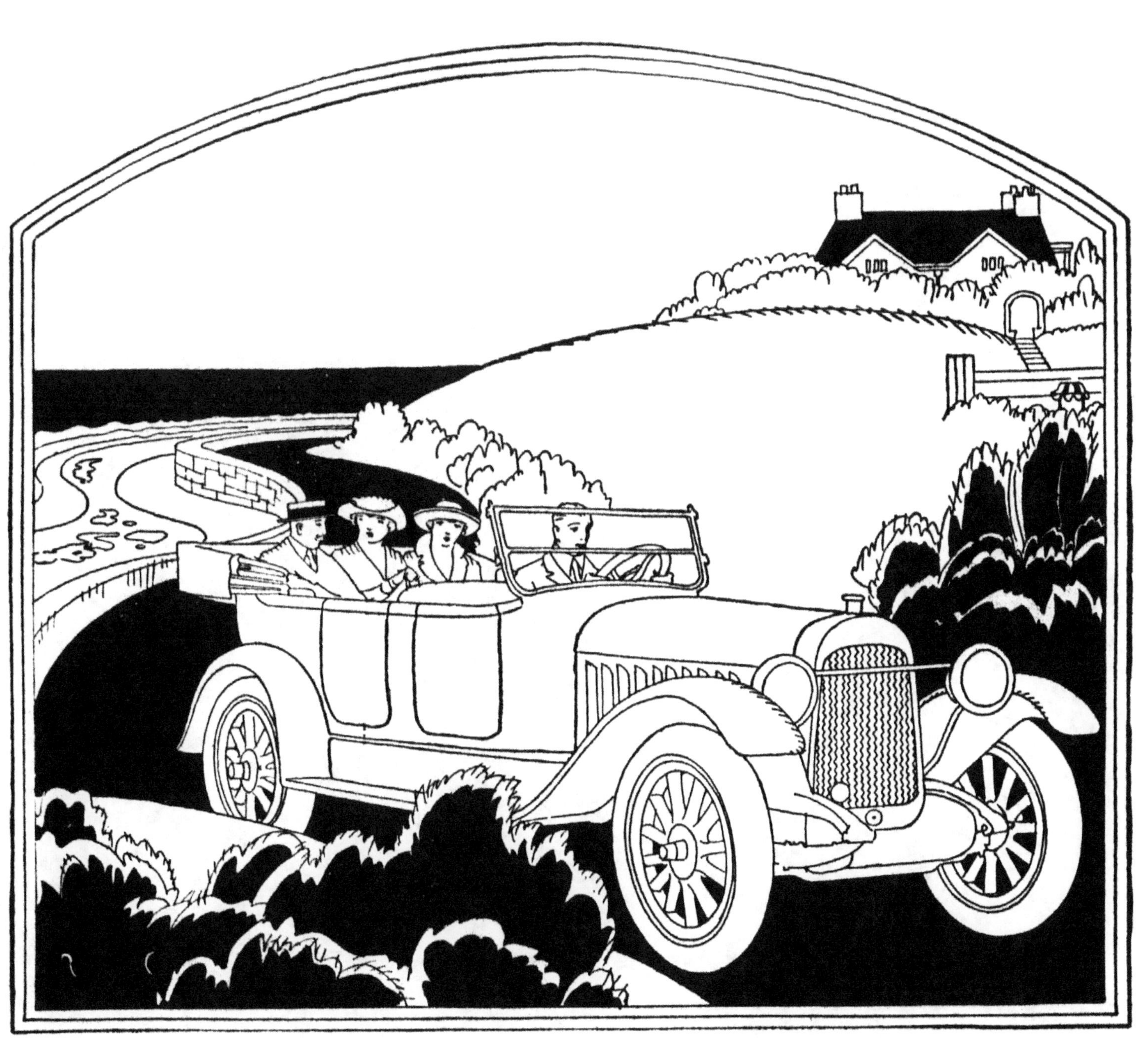

ABOUT THE ILLUSTRATION ON THE REVERSE

Automobile: Chalmers - Hot Spot

Original publication: Brooklyn Life (New York)

Publication date: March 29, 1919

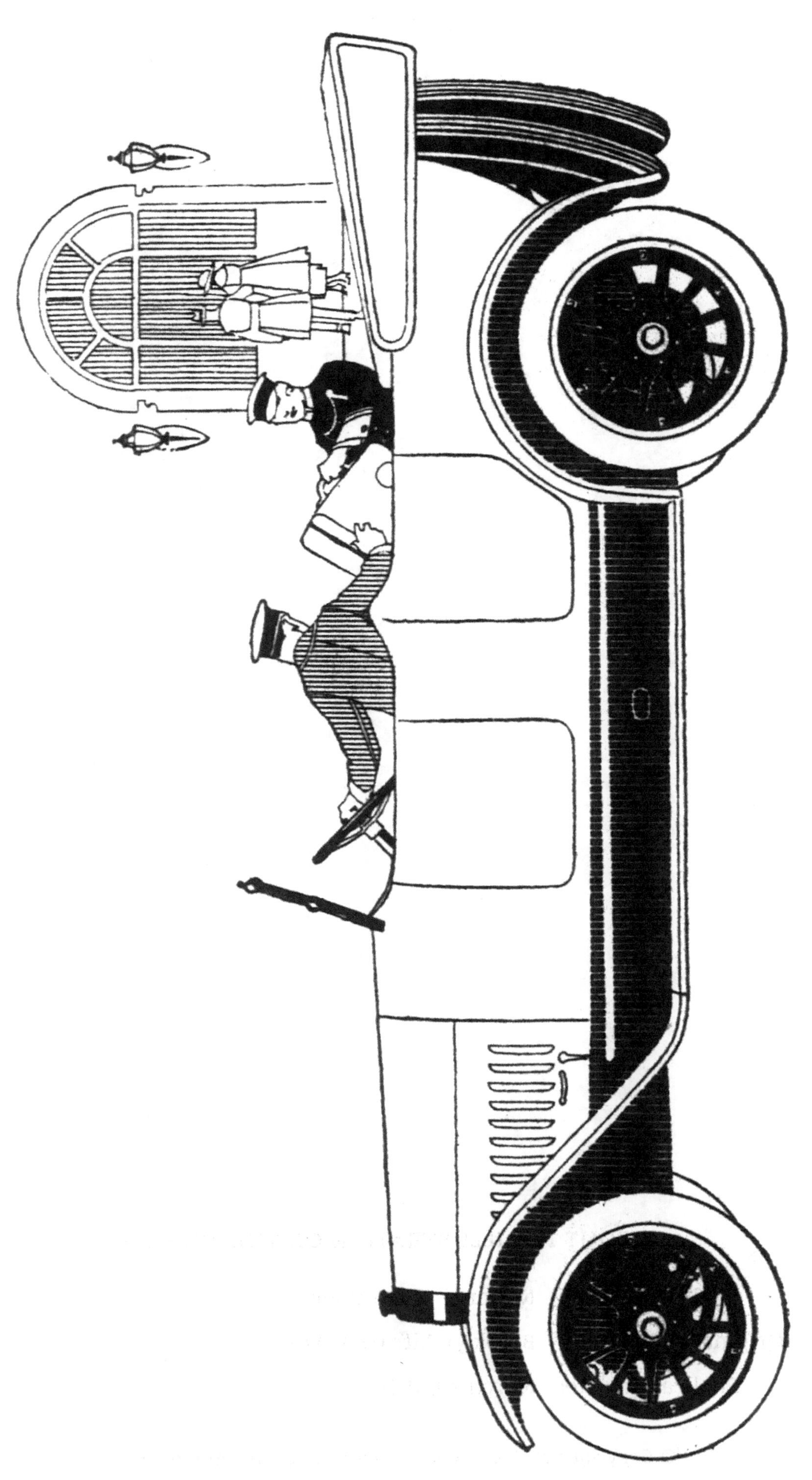

ABOUT THE ILLUSTRATION ON THE REVERSE

Automobile:	National 12-cylinder
Original publication:	Brooklyn Life (New York)
Publication date:	March 29, 1919

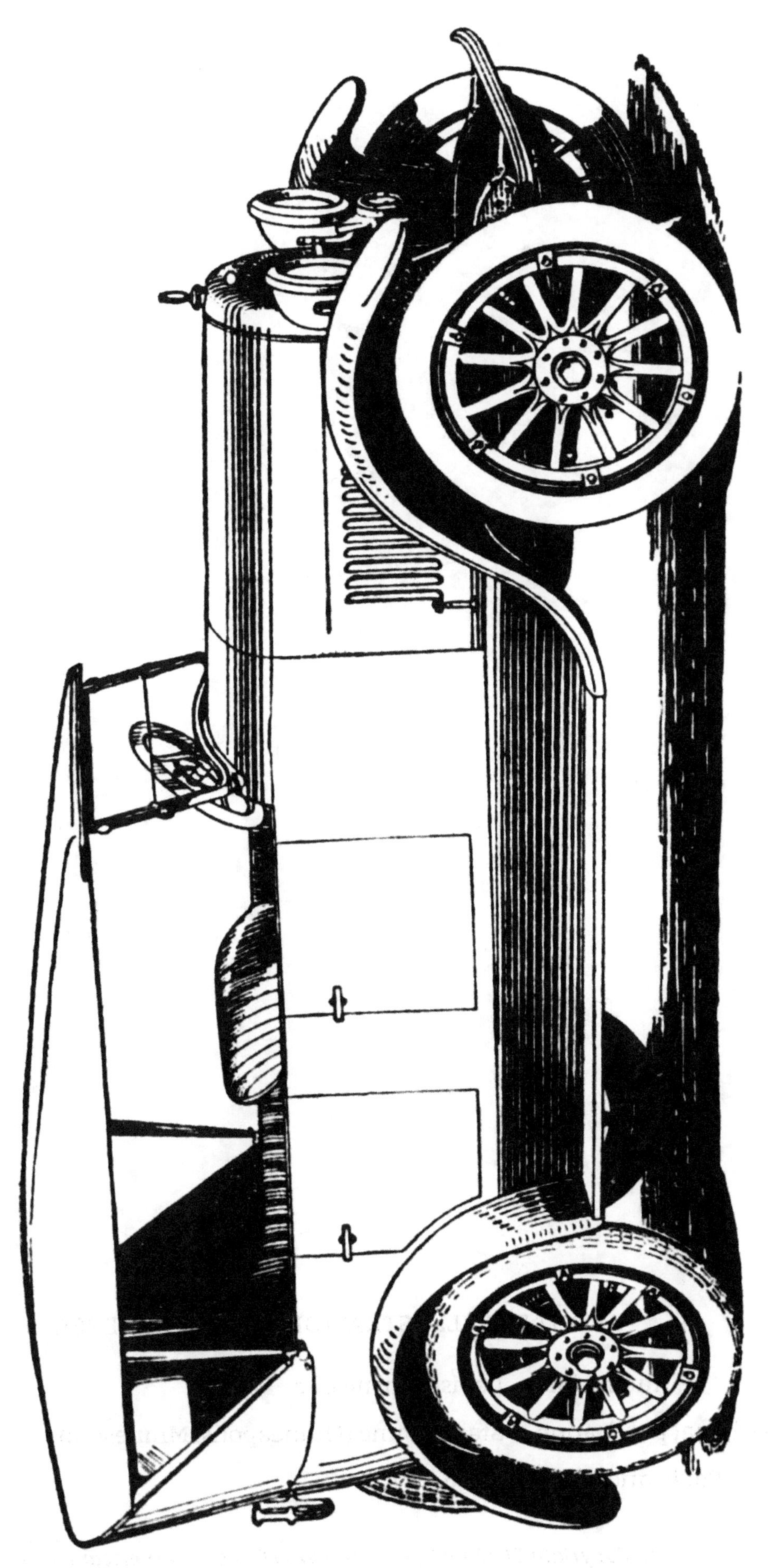

ABOUT THE ILLUSTRATION ON THE REVERSE

Automobile:	Davis Touring Car
Original publication:	Star Tribune (Minneapolis, Minnesota)
Publication date:	August 31, 1919

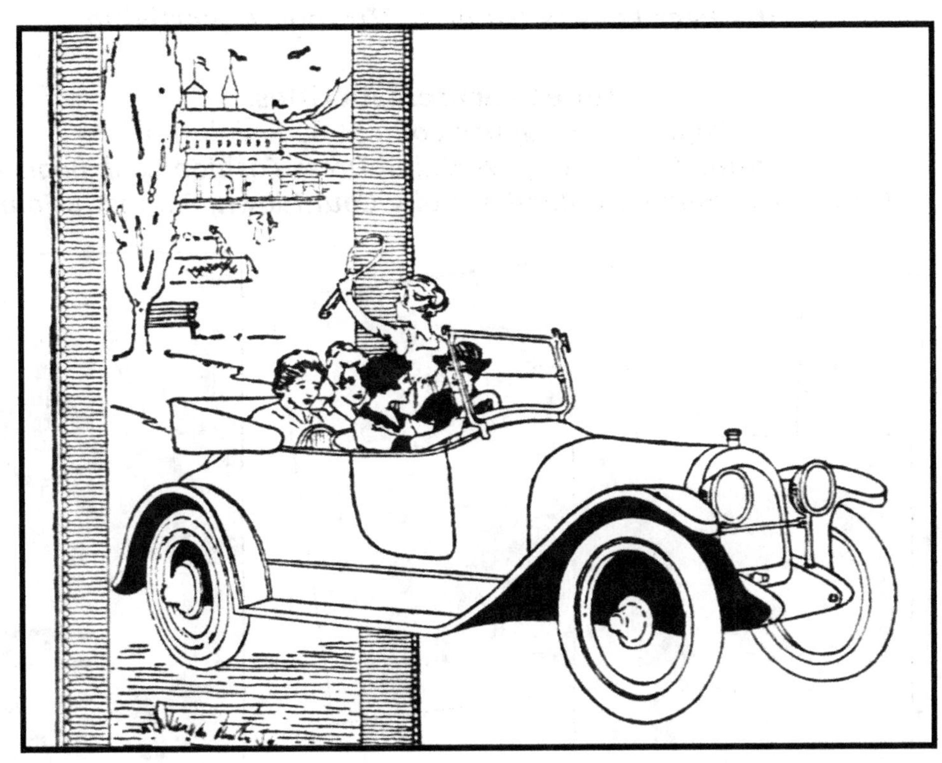

THE END

LIKE THIS BOOK? WE HAVE OTHERS!

Look for our *Classic Cars Adult Coloring Book* series!

And for more coloring, see...

If you're also a fan of history, check out our other books, including *Vintage Homes Adult Coloring Books, Vintage Women Adult Coloring Books* and *the Beer Lover's Guide to Vintage Advertising*

More Synchronista titles:
Pantsuits: Scrapbook of a Style Revolution
Something Old: Vintage Wedding Dress Fashion Look Book
All-In-One Pregnancy Calendar, Daily Countdown, Planner & Journal

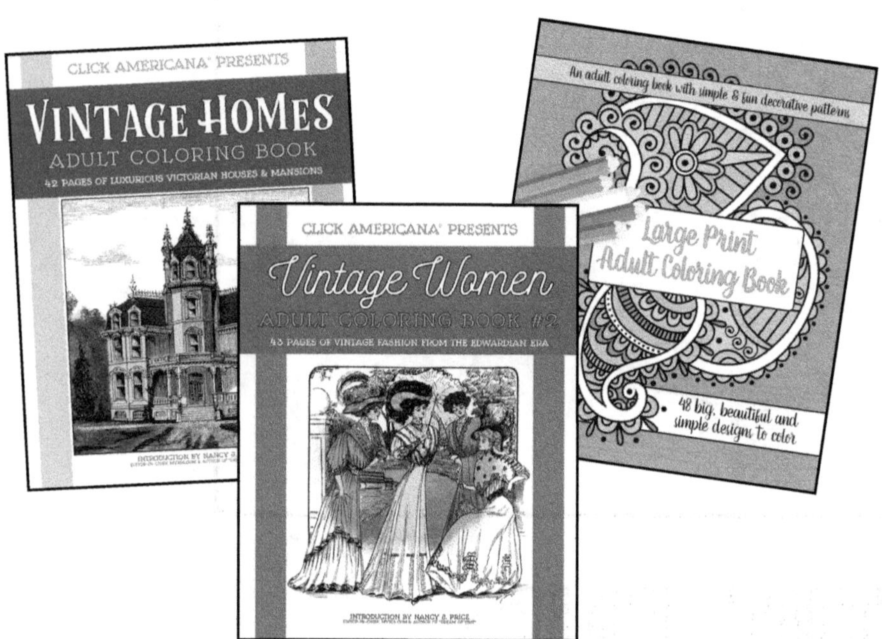

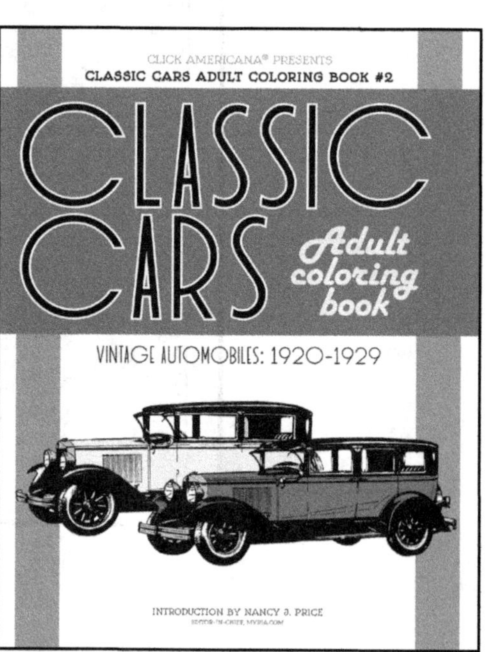

CHECK OUT OUR WEBSITES, TOO...

ClickAmericana.com
Thousands of articles, photos and vintage ads from throughout American history.

PrintColorFun.com
Hundreds of free coloring pages to download and print at home.

Myria.com
Smart stuff for real life:
Health, parenting, psychology, science, tech, entertainment — plus recipes, home decor & other good things.